Sheila's Guide
To
Lesser Sundra Islands, Indonesia
(Lombok, Sumbawa, Komodo, Rinca, Flores)

By
Sheila Simkin

Sheila Simkin, a native Chicagoan, has been traveling the world since 1960. The travel bug first hit on her honeymoon in Miami. Fidel Castro had just taken over Cuba and lured by rock-bottom prices, Sheila sweet-talked her then husband into abandoning Miami for Cuba. That marked the beginning of her lifetime travel passion and addiction.

There are very few countries that are **not** on her to-see list no matter how remote and/or difficult they may be. The U.S. State Department recognizes 193 independent countries and she has visited 150 in over 40 years of travel (but...who's **counting**). Touring, hiking, trekking, rafting, snowshoeing, skiing, volunteering on archaeological digs, family trips and, she must admit, occasionally sitting on a beach or compulsively shopping.

Travels With Sheila.com attempts to deliver the hard facts. Answer questions that will help you plan your holiday. Whether it be a tight or upscale budget, Sheila has probably been there...done it. She has built up a network of trusted tour operators who will plan an individualized trip and arrange treks for around the same price a group tour would charge. Perhaps, even for **less**. Sheila will give information about pensions, inns, hotels, train travel, air, adventures without sugarcoating.

Sheila is **not** a Travel Agent, has no affiliation with any agency or airline and tells it as she sees it. Her goal is to encourage you to take the big step and travel to more exotic, remote destinations by providing tips, anecdotes and reassurance that, yes, you will come back alive. Visit: www.TravelsWithSheila.com and Happy traveling.

INTRODUCTION

Indonesia is the largest island nation in the world, encompassing **17,000+** islands (Wouldn't you like to know who counted them?), each with its own unique culture. Previous visits to Java, Bali, Borneo and Sulawesi didn't **begin** to touch on the wonders Indonesia has to offer travelers. Indonesia is **inexpensive, if not downright cheap**, and filled with a panoply of unbelievable sights.

Why Visit the Lesser Sundra Islands? Lombok, Sumbawa, Komodo, Rinca and Flores are all part of the Lesser Sundra Islands, each known for different activities and sights. The main focus of those **in-the-know** is for a chance to spot the beyond impressive **Komodo Dragons**, the largest lizard on earth; vegetate on Lombok beaches; hike active volcanoes; snorkel and dive around the popular Gili Islands and Flores. **Please visit my travelswithsheila channel on YouTube.com to watch the videos.**

Let Travels With Sheila teach you how to **Travel on a Budget**, or go for broke and wallow in luxury on Lombok! Most importantly, let her ease your fears about languages, currencies, personal safety and **staying healthy.**

Are you ready to visit The Lesser Sundra Islands?

If so, you'll definitely be on the "road less traveled," smack in the middle of Indonesia's Ring of Fire. Sumbawa Island, for example, sees (perhaps) 60 tourists a year! Very few tourists are able to pry themselves away from fabulous Bali, a short boat ride away from Lombok, the most popular of the Lesser Sundras. Sheila's Guide to The Lesser Sundra Islands tells the good and the bad as **she** sees it, experienced by traveling from Lombok to Maumere, Flores, along with informative tips.

Sheila

PLANNING

Why have you decided to visit Indonesia's Lesser Sundra Islands? For the world renowned diving off Flores and around the Gili Islands? An in-depth cultural exploration? To see the Komodo dragons? A combination of all? Your decision determines **which** island you fly **into**, and which island you fly **out** of. We arranged a complete tour beginning in Lombok and finishing in Flores.

When to Go

The dry season, **May to October**. These islands have a tropical climate: sunny weather; year-round temperatures averaging 30 Celsius/86 Fahrenheit; two distinctive periods - the dry season and the rainy, wet season. Heed my advice! We visited in April and had constant rain! Climatologists are **serious** about statistics. Steve and I will never, and I do mean **never**, travel again without paying attention to climatic conditions. **May** is supposed to have the most perfect weather.

Air

International
International Flights land at Soekarno-Hatta Airport (CGK) in Jakarta. There are **no nonstop flights** from the U.S., U.K., or European Union countries. Countries within proximity to Indonesia do have nonstop flights. Your choice will be where to fly **into** before connecting onwards. Singapore was the closest gateway for us and had International flights from Singapore to Jakarta. I followed my advice below and turned in miles for Economy round-trip tickets from Singapore to Jakarta. **Indonesia airlines are so unsafe that the European Union banned them from flying to Europe!**

> **TIP**: Save your hard-earned miles for First or Business Class on long-distance flights (the only way we can afford to fly in those sections) and economy on short-hauls. It may only be 20,000 miles for a short-haul ticket.

Domestic
Garuda has been considered one of the **world's unsafest airlines**. That being said, we've safely flown on different airlines throughout Indonesia. A few Domestic Carriers are: Merpati, Lion Air, Batavia, Air Asia, and Express Air. It was an exercise in frustration trying to book on-line (Garuda repeatedly denied our credit card), and we finally paid a Travel Agent to do the ticketing. Warned by our tour operator that airlines returning to Denpasar from Maumere, Flores are notoriously undependable, and **cancel** at the drop of a hat, we built in extra days.

Public Bus/Local Transportation/Private Cars
We began this trip in Bali and flew from Denpasar to Lombok. Inter-island transport information will appear in each section of this Guide.

Less comfortable minibuses on each island are known locally as: *Bemos, Mikrolets* and *pete-petes* (intracity minibuses, carrying nine passengers). Destinations are written on a card in the front window. *Mikrolets* are sometimes called *Oplets* to make it even more confusing. Just wave down any vehicle that looks like it is going your way.

Becaks (bicycle rickshaws), shared taxis and *ojeks* will also vie for your business. *Ojek* is a method of motorcycle transport in which you pay the driver to ride on back of his motorcycle to your destination. It is also possible to rent your own motorcycle to get around.

Tour Operators

Travels With Sheila's current Indonesia go-to operators for private tours are: Caraka Travelindo (sulawesi-indonesia.com), Manado Safaris (manadosafaris.com), and Happy Trails (happytrailsindonesia.com) who arranged the Lesser Sundras. For the best in dive packages, contact Jeremy (a Dive Master) at Manado Safaris. They are reputable and arrange private, customized tours. **Travels With Sheila does not get freebies or discounts for recommending any tour operator**.

Surf the Internet and you'll see there is no shortage of tour operators who will arrange a vacation to your exact specifications. Or travel through the islands independently, using information in this Guide, and easily done if you have the time.

Hotels

Hotels on all islands from "luxury" on down (luxury is only found on Lombok), can easily be booked on commonly used websites. Tour Operators will arrange hotels throughout according to your budget. Independent travelers will always to find a home stay, or guesthouse without too much trouble. One hotel stay on Flores Island charged **$2.00 a night for two people, including breakfast!** How much lower can you go?

Currency

Rupiah (IDR) is the official currency. There is no problem exchanging GBP Sterling, Euros or U.S. Dollars in Indonesia but U.S. Dollars is the most preferred currency. There are ATMs in the major centers and moneychangers give the same rate without charging a commission. We needed very little cash since almost everything was included. In 2011, the Indonesia Rupiah exchange rate was: 8,995 Rupiah = $1 U.S. **Watch your zeros**: 89,955 = $10 U.S.; 899,555 = $100 U.S.

 TIP: Use a money belt, leave good jewelry at home and exercise caution.

Visas

Visas are required for all visitors to Indonesia, except for 11 countries eligible for a "Visa Free" entry. Check your nearest Indonesian Embassy for up-to-date information. U.S. Citizens can get a Visa On Arrival in Indonesia with a valid passport, onward or return tickets, and two color passport photos. There is a $25 U.S. charge for a 30-day visa.

Travel Insurance

Some don't buy travel insurance, we always do, just in case. Vacations are too costly to risk losing everything if any problems arise. Contact **Travel Guard** (travelguard.com) for insurance needs.

Health & Safety

I always check the **Centers for Disease Control** (cdc.gov) updates to see what they suggest. There is a risk of Malaria in Indonesia and Lariam (generic is Mefloquine) is the Malaria prophylaxis we use. A Tetanus booster is the most important inoculation in my estimation (we keep ours up-to-date religiously). It is not commonly known that you can get **Lockjaw** from contaminated dirt and even surface abrasions. Most people think that only a deep cut puts them at danger...not so. Hepatitis A and B are second on the list. Bring your other personal "drugs of choice."

> **TIP**: Antibiotics can be bought over-the-counter in Indonesia **without** a Doctor's prescription, but not "Controlled substances." Kimia Pharma carries high-quality drugs.

Even though bottled water is available throughout Indonesia, consider bringing iodine tablets for emergency purification situations. Don't even think of using tap water! **WASH YOUR HANDS...KEEP HANDS AWAY FROM EYES!** (ex-Marine, husband Steve, picked up a nasty eye infection in China.) Otherwise, cleanliness is next to Godliness when traveling.

Indonesia is currently safe to visit. Get up-to-date travel warnings from U.K. Foreign and Commonwealth Office (fco.gov.uk) and United States (travel.state.gov) websites.

Equipment

Cameras! Camcorder. Binoculars as well as a flashlight (torch) and Nalgene water bottles even though this was a cultural trip. **Flashlights** come in handy during cave visits, and power outages; they can even help you find the way from bed to bathroom. If the electricity ever fails during the night, you'll be happy to have a flashlight/ torch handy.

Clothing

Indonesia is hot and humid all year round. The dry season runs from May to November, wet season from December to April. A **hat**, long shorts/capris, T-shirts and sandals for every day....a very casual trip. A warm fleece or sweater for cool evenings. Lightweight boots for some of the day hikes; serious hiking equipment if climbing volcanoes.

What to See and Do in Lesser Sundra Islands

All pertinent information is inside this Guide.

Important Tips

⭐ Don't forget to call your ATM issuer and credit card companies, with international destination(s) information. Fraud, and identity theft, is at an all time high around the globe. You **don't** want the unpleasant surprise after handing over your credit card, or inserting your trusty ATM card in the machine, of seeing the nasty word "**DENIED**" pop up. It may not happen on your first transaction, but I'll bet a dozen doughnuts, it happens on the second. Make that telephone call to avoid embarrassment (and panic) upon hearing, "...so sorry, Madame, your card has been denied..."

⭐ Use an **ATM card for local currency** even if the bank tacks on a service charge. There are bancomats in 99% of the airports, railway stations, up and down streets, throughout the world.

⭐ **Do not,** under any circumstances, exchange money at home for your destination currency. The Euro is currently trading at 1.42 Euros to $1 U.S. In other words (because the Euro is confusing), it will cost you $1.42 U.S. to get 1 Euro. At almost all airport currency booths, it will cost you $1.62 to get 1 Euro, an additional 20 cents on each dollar. Additionally, do your very best to return home without any foreign currencies unless planning a return trip. Considering 2011 Currency Exchange Rates at O'Hare International Airport, you'll lose forty-two cents on every dollar. That's how banks and airport currency exchanges stay in business. Use those ATM cards!

⭐ Pack enough **batteries** for cameras, mobile phones, etc., and keep them charged throughout the trip. Indonesia is a feast of colorful sights.

⭐ **Internet** and Wi-Fi can be found in populated areas only.

⭐ Put cameras inside **plastic bags** to protect from road dust; pack all clothing in luggage **inside** large, plastic garbage bags;

⭐ Pack an **extra pair of glasses**. ex-Marine forgot his on the Annapurna Sanctuary Trek in Nepal. First, one earpiece broke off, followed by the other earpiece the next day. Unable to see without his glasses, we **DUCT-TAPED** the earpieces on each day.

⭐ **Don't** eat perishable **food** that's been sitting in the sun and/or outside all day. Food poisoning occurs in clean restaurants too, not just in Indonesia, but throughout the world. Conversely, don't be afraid to eat in local restaurants along the road - **if** they are crowded, and **if** your guide assures food safety. It's some of the best food you'll ever taste at rock-bottom prices.

⭐ Make **copies of passport**.

⭐ **Duct tape**. Duct tape can be your best friend in an emergency. It will hold boots together (seriously, been there, done that...), and patch anything. There are non-ending uses for duct tape and you'll make the locals happy by leaving the roll behind.

⭐ Bring your favorite **snacks/munchies** with from home or buy along the road to eat on long car journeys, and when you arrival someplace at an unexpected, ungodly hour, starving to death.

⭐ Don't forget **earplugs**. Useful in even the best hotels as protection against very loud guests. I never leave home without them.

Welcome to Lombok, Sumbawa, Komodo, Rinca and Flores Islands, Indonesia!

INDONESIA INFORMATION AND TRIVIA

Indonesia is the biggest Muslim country in the world with approximately **250,000,000 Muslims** followed by Pakistan and India;

Indonesia has some of the most **active volcanoes in the Pacific Ring of Fire.** Several are: Kelut and Merapi on Java; and Mt. Soputan, Sulawesi (around 60 kilometers/36 miles from Manado);

The majority of tourists come from Holland, Spain, France, Germany and Australia;

Indonesia has **100 snake species**, Rhinoceros, Tiger and Leopard (all three of these very rare)

Indonesians want to be a politician because of graft, looting and easy money; Jakarta is the epicenter of the "job Mafia." There are 34 political parties in Indonesia (**and we think we have problems**). Political nominees distribute **free food** to anyone who shows up at their rallies, creating massive traffic jams in every village we went through. Wouldn't **you** for a free meal;

Horse-drawn carts are called *Bendi*. If there aren't any blue cars (shared taxis), or public buses near villages, locals use *Bendi;*

Indomaret's are all over Indonesia, a "7-11" type of mini-mart with low prices. Shop here for water, cosmetics, munchies, even c.d.'s;

Wanita means "Woman" - important to know when faced with two bathrooms;

If you need any kind of prescription medicine, go to the nearest **Kimia Farma**, a chain of clean and dependable pharmacies. You **do not need a Doctor's prescription** in Indonesia, the pharmacist and assistants usually speak English and medication is reasonable in price;

Internet is cheap in Indonesia, usually around 50 cents for one hour;

Warungs and *Restos* are either small, family owned restaurants or larger restaurants. Food is very inexpensive in Indonesia and it's difficult to spend more than **$5.00 U.S.** per person for a really filling meal, tax and tip included;

If you rent a motorbike, be forewarned that Indonesian police **constantly** stop riders to show identification just to **fine them**. Call it a scam, bribe, shakedown or all the above;

Long distance buses drive from Jakarta all the way to Flores for around $30 U.S. The buses drive straight through. Drivers relieve each other, passengers sleep on the bus and/or on the ferry crossings that can take more than five hours;

It is **extremely**, and I do mean **extremely**, easy to arrange ongoing travel once you arrive, and tour operators give discounts!

Food: Don't be surprised to see cobra, python, cat, rat, dog, bat and buffalo on menus in restaurants;

Try to do the "rough stuff" first when planning a trip **before** booking "nicer" hotels; it's a huge culture shock to begin in hotels/inns/guesthouses and end sleeping on floors; and

A few words to know before you go: *Terima kasih* = "thank you"; *Hati-Hati* = "careful"; and *Sama-sama* = "you are welcome".

LOMBOK ISLAND: KNOW BEFORE YOU GO

Lombok forms part of the Lesser Sundra Islands and is separated from Bali on the West by the Lombok Strait, and Alas Strait between it and Sumbawa to the East. Indonesia has 16,000-17,000 islands, depending who you listen to, and a population of over **300 million people**! It's not surprising that tourism is the most important industry here with gorgeous beaches ranging from white sand to black volcanic sand. The most developed area is on the West coast of the island, centered on Senggigi, and caters to backpackers along with luxury seekers.

Kuta in **South Lombok** has some of the best surfing in the world according to a leading surfing magazine and magnificent stretches of tranquil, white sand beaches. **This is not Kuta, Bali**. Lombok is rapidly turning into a second Bali so get here now. If you prefer a livelier atmosphere, wait for more development.

Lombok is a popular destination for three reasons: the famous Gili Islands; Mount (Gunung) Rinjani for trekkers who spend the night on top of the volcano; and surfing.

Transportation

Lombok Island is easy to access from Bali, the most commonly used jumping off point. There are Domestic flights from Jakarta, Sumbawa, Flores; International flights from Singapore and Malaysia.

> **TIP**: Check and recheck all the information below for up-to-date advice from travel agents in Bali! Schedules are constantly changing.

Bali to Lombok by Boat
Large and slow ferries (4-5 hours) travel between Padangbai in East Bali to Lembar, Lombok every 90 minutes around the clock. Or take one of the speedy BlueWater Express catamarans from Serangan in South Bali (closer to the Kuta Beach area) that first stops at Gili Trawangan before continuing to Teluk Kode on the Lombok mainland.

Bali to Lombok by Air
Denpasar International Airport has two separate terminals, Domestic and International with the same routine in both. Show tickets to enter, check luggage with no weight requirements, and pay 40,000 IDR (less than $5 U.S.) per person passenger fee (**must be in Rupiah**). Security is semi-thorough: water bottles are allowed; no 3 x 3 x 3 ounce rule; leave shoes on and computers in your carry on.

There are daily flights from Denpasar to the new **Lombok International Airport** on airlines that you've probably never heard of: Merpati (seven daily), Wings Air (four daily) and GT Air (two daily); Trigana Air; besides Garuda and IAT. This new airport replaced Selaparang Airport, closer to Mataram in 2011. Lombok International Airport has a single terminal building to handle both International and Domestic flights. The city of Mataram is approximately 40 kilometers/25 miles northwest of the airport; public buses and taxis to both Mataram and Senggigi are your best bet.

There are tour desks, booking kiosks and other facilities to assist travelers in Lombok International Airport.

The Gili Islands

The three, highly popular Gili Islands lie only 1-5 kilometers/.6-3.1 miles off the mainland. The closest Gili Island is Gili Air while laid back Gili Meno is between Gili Air and Gili Trawangan. Gili Trawangan is "Party Central"; the largest and most visited with something always happening. Boats usually stop at all three islands.

Lombok Transport to the Gili Islands
Public boats from Bangsal near Pemenang; and/or Private chartered boats from Senggigi or Teluk Nare.

Local boats will take up to 10 people between the Gili Islands and over to mainland Lombok. There are also island hopping services that leave at set times.

Bali Transport to the Gili Islands:
Gili Cat (gilicat.com) between Padangbai to Gili Trawangan; Blue Water Express (bwsbali.com) leaves from both Padangbai and Serangan; and Various charters.

> **TIP**: Boating **anywhere** in Indonesian waters is fraught with danger: overloaded ferries and small boats; no life vests (or not enough life vests); total disregard of weather; and rough seas, to name a few. Carefully pick your operator and be aware of weather.

Mount Rinjani

Lombok's other big draw is Mount Rinjani for adventure seekers who hike to the crater lake. If you are serious about this, umpteen tour operators will be glad to arrange. Visit the Mount Rinjani website(rinjaninationalpark.com) for detailed information. **This hike is not a cakewalk!** Prepare for either: 2 Days/1 Night with camping in a forest or meadow depending on where you stop; 3 Days/2 Nights hike; or go for broke and head to the summit on a 4 Day/3 Night climb. How many nights do you want to spend sleeping on top of a volcano? For us, **zero**. Lombok's topography is dominated by this stratovolcano, the second highest volcano in Indonesia. It last erupted in May, 2010 when lava flowed into the caldera lake.

LOMBOK INFORMATION AND TRIVIA

Lombok has a tropical climate with warm and humid weather all year round. Wet season, **November-April**; Dry Season, **May-October.** May in the best month with almost perfect weather;

Lombok is the most popular destination for three reasons: the famous Gili Islands; Mount (Gunung) Rinjani for trekkers who spend the night on top of the volcano; and surfing;

Lombok population is over 3 million, Islam is the main religion, and 90% of the people are of Sasak origin. The Sasak people mix basic Islamic beliefs along with Hindu-Buddhist beliefs. This created the Wetu Telu religion. (More about how they co-mingle later in this Guide.);

Lombok has three main districts with three capital cities: Mataram in the West, Praya in central and Selong in east Lombok. The majority of commerce is in the capital city of Mataram in west Lombok;

If you plan traveling around the island and visiting small villages, it is more respectable to wear slacks or knee length shorts, a shirt with sleeves or a sarong; and

The island of Lombok shapes up at about 80 kilometers/50 miles from east to west, and the same from north to south, with lush evergreen landscapes, volcanoes, and parts which are chronically dry.

LOMBOK ISLAND, THE GATEWAY TO THE LESSER SUNDRAS

Happiness is arriving at Soekarno-Hatta Airport, Jakarta (or **anywhere** you travel) **with all your luggage**. Get an easy, Visa On Arrival - Passports, two passport-sized photographs, $25 - before continuing through Immigration. When you exit, a row of booths line walls to exchange money. Definitely exchange some money if an ATM isn't available. You'll need Rupiahs to use for Domestic Departure Taxes (more about that below). Garuda or Merpati customers can then walk from the International side of the terminal over to the Domestic side for check-in.

All other airlines require a **terminal change on the free bus**. After clearing customs, follow signs that say, "Passengers using buses and taxis" outside the terminal. You'll see a stairwell on your left after exiting with a lift opposite. Take the lift to Level 2, exit, turn left, and walk a short distance to a blue and white sign which says, "Shuttle Bus Stop." Buses come about every 10 minutes. Don't hesitate to ask someone if the above still holds true! Airports are constantly in flux.

> **TIP**: There are **Domestic departure taxes**, 30,000 Rupiah per person (02/2012)!

Oops! Standing at the Garuda Airlines counter, check-in personnel informed us that we had to pay **Domestic departure taxes** and we hadn't changed any **money**. He took our dollars even though taxes are "supposed" to be paid in Rupiah, adding on a little "extra" for himself.

> **TIP**: I **always** recommend packing **everything** in your suitcase **inside plastic** (we use big garbage bags). Haven't you ever seen suitcases sitting on the tarmac during a snowstorm or heavy rain? A good thing we did because my suitcase came off the conveyor belt, **sopping wet**. Who knows "Why," but everything inside stayed dry.

We began, and would end, the Lesser Sundra trip in Bali. Cendana Resort & Spa, Ubud transferred us back to Denpasar International Airport after hearty breakfast with cheese *jaffles* (fritter like yummies that resemble a Pop Tart). Allow plenty of time for your ride to the airport. It took a **slow** 1-1/2 hours to go 50 kilometers/30 miles. Even the driver was getting nervous!

It was a sunny day, good for a 20-minute, low altitude flight on a prop jet. Guide Nasip and driver, Mr. Parhan were waiting at the Mataram Airport in Lombok with a sign and off we drove to the Hotel Graha Beach Senggigi, only about 20 minutes away. (Lombok now has a new airport and Mataram Airport has closed.)

Senggigi

Senggigi is the most developed tourist area along the 30 kilometer/20 mile strip of coastal road north of Mataram. This road continues to Bangsal, port for the Gili Islands. Most travelers start or end their stay at Senggigi because of easy access to the Airport and accommodation options. If you take the slow ferry from Bali, it is advisable to book with a tour operator for transport because the Lombok dock is in a remote area, several kilometers south of Mataram.

Downtown Senggigi has restaurants, bars, discotheques, travel agents, money changers, and a range of accommodations from budget guest houses to five-star hotels. Restaurants and small cafes line the colorful main beach road, and swimming off the beach is safe. Steve and I were looking forward to walking into Senggigi for a good browse.

Questions for guide Nasip, whether or not we needed boots, sarong and temple scarves for tomorrow's visit to Pura Lingsar Temple. On an earlier trip through Java and Bali, we had to carry a sarong and temple scarf to visit all temples. None of these are needed in Lombok; Temples **lend** a temple scarf for a pittance and that is sufficient. Repack the sarong and boots.

Hotel Graha Beach Senggigi

Hotel Graha Beach Senggigi (grahasenggigi.com) is set on a wide stretch of white sandy beach. A short 30 minute ride from Mataram, the hotel was set on both sides of the highway and looked beautiful when our driver pulled in. Then, they showed us our **room**. Happy Trails booked us into standard rooms throughout the Lesser Sundra exploration. That is not be a problem but this particular room was not only hideously shabby, but also fronted a very busy highway. With two nights here, I gave ex-Marine **"the look"** and sent him back across the highway to see what other rooms were available.

He returned with a bellman and news they were moving us two rooms away from the highway. This room was even smaller and uglier than the first. Another **"look"** along with instructions to upgrade us if possible. Graha Beach Senggigi has Standard Rooms (550 IDR/$50 U.S.), and Superior Rooms (650 IDR/$65 U.S.) on the beach side. Deluxe Rooms (750 IDR/$75 U.S.) on the other side. Restaurants on both sides. This time the man got smart and **inspected** another room before returning. Schlepped the suitcases back across the highway, past the swimming pool, to a deluxe cottage with a large, beautiful room, twice the size of the Standard Room; a little garden area, and shower open to the elements for an additional $20 U.S. per night. Travels With Sheila now had a "happy look" on her face and ex-Marine had a "happy look" because he had done something right.

Downtown Senggigi was within easily walkable distance, 1 kilometer/.6 mile but, guess what. It began to rain. Oh, what the hell, a torrential downpour; sheets of rain, thunder, and lightening from 2:00p through most of the night! That put the kibosh on enjoying the beautiful white sand beach or walking to town. Fortunately, every room had a big umbrella for guests' use.

Amenities and services at The Graha Beach Senggigi? Two computers in the lobby area for free Internet access, next to the Naga Restaurant that served Oriental cuisine. Free transport to and from the Airport; satellite TV with in-house video; hot and cold running water; air conditioning that was so powerful we froze to death during the night; and the open air Graha Restaurant on the beach. A good thing there were restaurants since guide Nasip dropped us off, and **disappeared**. This is a cardinal boo-boo when traveling, and I should know better. Have your guide inspect the room first, give a cell/mobile phone number, and don't let him/her **leave** until you have clear information what is happening. Bad Sheila!

Menus were in the room for both restaurants, and the beachside restaurant looked more appealing. Grabbed the umbrella, tip toed over wet marble floors, across the highway and ordered. A whole chicken, French fries, egg rolls and a beer to split. Neither of us could believe our eyes when the "whole chicken dish" was placed on the table. (A **sparrow** would have been bigger than that poor chicken, all bones.) **And**, there was a small **chicken head** in the middle of the plate. That did it. Instant loss of appetite. Covered the plate with a napkin and snarfed down fries, too grossed out to even take a photograph. A terrible, terrible dinner and if that was any indication of food quality, we'd buy bread rolls and eat tuna sandwiches; tuna pouches travel the world with us.

Breakfast began at 7:00a, in the same restaurant. A decent buffet with eggs made to order, tempera style vegetables (greasy but tasty), noodles, rice, juice, fresh fruit and good coffee. Not a chicken head in sight, vendors walked up and down the beach selling pearls and T-shirts, much better...

WHAT TO SEE AND DO ON LOMBOK ISLAND

Unique Pura Lingsar Temple

Pura Lingsar Temple is sacred and unique because it blends two religions: Wetu Telu, a combination of Adat and Islam, practiced by the Sasak people, Lombok's natives; and Balinese Hinduism. The Sasak people adopted beliefs from Hinduism but kept their native animistic traditions even though they still consider themselves Muslim. Pura Lingsar is Lombok's most important religious site as well as main tourist attraction. The temple was built in 1714 by Balinese Hindus when they first visited Lombok.

Guide Nasip and driver picked us up at Hotel Graha Beach Senggigi and we headed south through Mataram before turning east to Pura Lingsar Temple. Nasip is not allowed to enter Lombok tourist attractions because local guides have a lock on showing tourists around. He turned us over to guide Udah who began a rapid fire introduction to Pura Lingsar. It was easy to see that he was determined to show us around quickly, get rid of us, and go on to the next tourist. He began explanations in front of two gorgeous ponds filled with water lilies/lotus blossoms. One pond symbolized Bali while the other symbolized Lombok. Each also had statues of twin brothers along with a long, boring story.

A 5,000 Rupiah donation to the temple allowed us use their yellow temple scarves to tie around waists. Temple scarves function to divide the upper body and mind with sacred thoughts, from lower body sexual thoughts. The temple also sold **hard-boiled eggs** to feed the **holy eels**. Udah was unenthusiastic about buying eggs. "You have to get a priest to unlock the pond gate. You have to pay for the eggs. The eels may not come out of their hole." With that, we left the eggs behind and entered Pura Lingsar.

We had just missed a buffalo sacrifice. Not that I enjoy watching a buffalo get his throat slashed while blood gushes all over, but rituals are interesting. A live buffalo and a goat were tethered on the temple grounds happily chomping grass. (Little did they know this would be their last meal; on the to-be slaughtered list.) Locals bring their **own** sacrifices to the temple, cook the meat and **hang** the animal heads by a holy well (filled with "holy eels") inside the inner courtyard. The freshly butchered buffalo stunk! Other local Sasak were busy preparing even **more** offerings; chickens "sacrificed" at home, brought to Pura Lingsar, grilled and served on a bed of rice. Some to eat, some to offer. **They** smelled pretty darn good.

The northern, elevated part of the temple was the Hindu section with the Wetu Telu section in the South. Don't even ask which was which. Udah confused the living hell out of me describing Hindu and Sasak Muslim customs. However, the most interesting sights in Pura Lingsar had to do with the **Wetu Telu** beliefs:

- The "holy eels," holed up in the "holy pond," and sacred to Vishnu;

- A row of "holy" rocks garbed in white and yellow brought by a king (whomever he was) with more sacrifices in front of them. Children are brought to this place for circumcision rituals; and

- A "holy spring" with separate areas for women and men to bathe.

To add even more confusion to the mix, the **Chinese** also come here to worship. **They** sacrifice a **goat,** take the goat's head and place it on their **automobile** for about 30 minutes. Can you imagine seeing a car with a goat's head on it? **That** would have been the ultimate sight!

A tip to ungracious Udah who didn't even say, "Thank you." It's an old story. Whatever you give is never enough for some people.

Taman Narmada, Pottery and Rattan Craft Villages

Taman Narmada Complex was built in 1805 by the Rajah of Mataram. When he became too old to climb Rinjani Volcano to throw offerings into the holy lake, he had a replica of Rinjani with its crater lake built. It is a miniature replica and was touted as a special place to spend a few hours. We said, **bor---ing** and spent five minutes here before moving along.

There are two main pottery villages that tourists visit: Masbagik and Banyumulek, around 14 kilometers/9 miles south of Mataram. Banyumulek is the bigger one with rows of art shops selling products. Women are the potters in this area of Lombok; unusual since we've always seen just men making pottery. Women pass down their pottery-making skills to daughters, showing them how to work the clay by hand. I love pottery. Enjoy seeing it made but go ahead, ask me, "Have you ever watched pottery being made, Sheila?" Umm...yes. In Orissa, Thailand, Morocco, and Little Rann of Kutch (a few months ago). Totally potterey'd out, we passed on yet another pottery village and continued to Beleka, a **rattan village**. At least we had never seen rattan woven before.

Beleka has been supplying Jakarta and Bali with rattan products for decades. I didn't discover until later that Beleka had antique shops and art shops in the village who sold to individuals. Beleka was another hour's ride, and silly me thought there would be a big cooperative showing **how** they wove rattan along with shops **selling** the finished product; wrong. The driver parked on a street, and we began walking from house to house, down narrow alleys with chickens and pigs, looking for women who sat outside houses weaving rattan.

What is Rattan? Rattan is the name for roughly 600 species of palm trees. Rattan is a good material because it is lightweight, durable, and flexible. The core of Rattan is used in furniture making. We watched different women take strands of rattan, peel off the skin, and then pull more strands through a heavy, metal disk with holes. Fine pieces of grass were used to "sew" larger pieces of rattan together. It takes two to three days to complete one item, everything they were working on had been commissioned, and a huge truck, overloaded with goods, was heading to Jakarta with rattan products

Two interesting rattan facts:

- Rattan is used for **"Caning"** (whipping for disciplinary pain) because of its flexibility; and

- Italian scientists are currently experimenting with Rattan to produce **artificial bone**! The bone is currently being tested in sheep, with implants into humans anticipated to start in 2015.

Watching a woman manipulate thin, sharp pieces of rattan and grass, I asked how badly her hands get cut up. Nasip asked. The woman answered, **"Beats working in the fields."**

How true...

The Friendly Weaving Village of Sukarara

Two different weaving villages are part of itineraries in this area of Lombok: Pringgasela and Sukarara. Nasip seemed to feel that Sukarara was a little less "touristy." Local guide, "Sam" took us on a walk through quiet Sukarara. A wedding would take place later today, and almost the entire village was involved in wedding preparations; sitting in the village center eating, cooking and schmoozing. Men did the cooking for the wedding feast; turning bananas into cooked vegetables, adding wonderfully smelling spices, and filling huge pots with rice.

Even though these people are Muslim, traditional animist beliefs prevail with one of those being: women may give a "look" or something else that would **curse the food if they did the cooking.** Hmmm... Women of the world, unite; tell males in your household that you'll **curse** the food by cooking and see how that goes. **But** women were allowed to **wash all the dishes** and dry a mixture of rice cakes in the sun for the wedding "cake," given to guests in individual pieces.

Sukarara also had multiple Shamans. One for healing, another who used magic to drive away evil, plus a few more with other responsibilities. The people in Sukarara Village were extremely friendly, wanted photos taken, and had questions for us. Sam translated, since he spoke English, into their native dialect. Indonesia has a gazillion different dialects and even **they** don't always understand each other.

We walked down the road to an area with a rice granary, and communal shop where all weavings are sold made by this cooperative. Sukarara (pop: 8,000) is known for its beautiful cloth produced from natural cottons and dyes. All women in Sukarara weave **without exception**. They begin learning around seven years of age and aren't even allowed to **marry** until they know how to weave. I asked Sam what happens if a girl is totally uncoordinated (like me) and just **can't** weave. He replied, "There is no choice. A woman will work with her until she learns."

One woman left the pre-wedding festivities to demonstrate weaving. She set up her Backstrap Loom in a raised bamboo shelter, and began to weave while Sam answered questions.

A Backstrap Loom is deceptively simple. For the most part, it consists of sticks, rope, and a strap that is worn around the weaver's waist, hence the name, "Backstrap." Backstrap looms are simple to use and weave at. They can be set up indoors or outside, and adjusted to fit the weaver. Each woman in Sukarara makes her own loom, washes and dyes cotton with natural colorings like tamarind juice, indigo and other root extracts.

It had been a long, interesting day but we were hot, tired and ready to leave. Sam insisted we visit the cooperative showroom and then wound a sarong around me to make me into an Indonesian Bride. There was no way I could get out of it without creating an international incident, it was **not** one of my finest hair days (as if I ever **have** a good hair day) plus sweat was flying in all directions. I looked like a lumpy, dumpy Indonesian bride with no redeeming qualities. So terrible that you'll have to watch the video to see what I mean. It took ages before I could persuade Sam to unroll me from the sarong and let me go. Sorry, Sam I am....

There's Gold in The Hills

Another roadside stop after Nasip told us about "gold fever" in this part of Lombok. Not only gold but copper, silver and other ores. There are a few big mining companies extracting ores legally, but all you have to do is drive along Lombok roads listening for machine noise. Countless and deafening tumblers rotate in front of houses crushing ore-laden rocks. Those rocks, and Lombok, are **loaded** with gold. Hundreds of families have caught gold fever; "panning" for gold, digging illegal mine tunnels and dragging hundreds of bags filled with rocks out of the mountains daily.

We stood and watched a family group process ore. They travel daily to their own secret site in the mountains and fill at least four bags of rocks. These rocks (ore) are then put in a mechanical, noisy tumbler that spins and crushes the rocks for four hours. A tumbler full of crushed rock is removed, and a small amount dumped in a pan filled with water and mercury. Mercury is supposed to pick up the finest gold in the pan but is also toxic. This is where what I refer to as the " gold panning" process began. He slowly began swirling rocks around, picking up and throwing out big pieces of rock and gravel until only silt remained in the bottom of the pan. Sounds easy but was laborious, and time consuming. Local then took this "silt," put in a cloth and began wringing it out. After squishing for a few minutes, he opened the cloth and son of a gun, there was a tiny white piece of gold.

There has been a big brouhaha over illegal gold mining in Lombok. People process gold in plain sight of authorities next to the road, and are getting **rich**. Many die when illegal mining tunnels collapse, but the mercury is what would concern me. These men have their hands in a concentration of water and mercury all day. Surely, mercury poisoning will set in eventually. And what about mercury leaching into their groundwater and rivers? Frightening!

A Small Village Wedding

"Travel" for us is all about meeting people around the world. Learning about their lives, and families. Visiting villages, tasting different foods (pass on the greasy, deep fried tarantulas). A supreme happening is an unexpected encounter with a local funeral, wedding, religious rite or other family occasion. I've learned to **tell guides** what we like to see and do before they drag us to five consecutive churches or go into a 30-minute description of the **330 Million Hindu Gods**, and suggest you do the same. With that in mind, Nasip had news that a local wedding was taking place today not far from where he lived. Were we interested? Do bears s--t in the woods? I'm always up for a wedding.

An Indonesian wedding is a very important event. Whether you live in a small village or large town, people that are even **slightly** acquainted with the bride and groom are invited. Mr. Parhan parked the car on a dirt road where a few, traditionally dressed men sat, and we began walking on mud, along a stream towards loud music. Women and children were standing in front of a tent enclosure waiting for the bride and groom while men were out in back, cooking up huge pots of food. Remember the Sukarara village wedding preparations where women are believed to **cast evil spells** if they do the wedding cooking? It was the same here.

This was the **bride's** village. She and her groom would lead a procession later today to the groom's village, Gamelon music playing while all the guests followed. This couple was married about a month ago, but it takes time to settle intricate details and plan festivities. The family of the bridal couple was helping them into traditional Indonesian finery in a small house, a short distance from the tent. The bride's beautiful little sister was having make-up applied, and the family graciously allowed us to enter, take photographs and wish them well.

Dressed for the occasion, the bridal party was escorted to the decorated tent, and took their places up front while huge amplifiers, band and wedding singer welcomed guests on behalf of the bride's family.

The extremely friendly villagers had just finished a big lunch and were very excited to see us join the festivities. Unlike countries where tourists are expected to pay for photographs, Indonesian people almost **begged** us to take their pictures. What would I have done without a digital camera? Click, delete, click, delete...

We were invited to return at 4:00p and join the procession to the groom's village, but after watching gold mining, rattan making, weaving and visiting temples, total exhaustion had set in. You can't do it all!

A long day filled with many different sights. Starving by now, we drove back to Mataram and into a great bakery urged on by Nasip who said this was going to be the last place to stock up on goodies in Lombok. There is only one large bakery in Mataram; ask locals where it it. Delicious cakes in tummies, we revived enough to visit a wholesale T-shirt shop that supposedly sells to all the vendors, who sell to you, the tourist. Sad to say, these T-shirts were just as expensive as the ones sold along the beach!

Senaru, at The Base of Mount Rinjani

It was only a two-hour ride from Senggigi to Senaru, the jumping off point for treks up Mount (Gunung) Rinjani. The beautiful drive ran along the coast heading to north Lombok with occasional stops; black volcanic sand beaches, and Bangsal. There is a pearl farming industry off the coast but visits aren't allowed, and no one sells pearls on the beach; the pearls are all taken to Mataram - disappointing.

Bangsal Harbor is a small, forsaken spot on a black, volcanic beach where public and private boats from all three **Gili Islands** dock (more information in this Guide's Planning Chapter). There is **nothing** around, and I do mean **nothing.** No taxis. No transport. Make all your Gili Island arrangements through travel agents and tour operators who drop off and pick up clients. For hotel information, check out the following websites: hotels.com, booking.com, hostelbookers.com, and gili-paradise.com (also with helpful Gili information). All motorized transport is banned on the Gilis. To get around, use feet, or a horse-drawn cart.

Small boats were loading perishables, and gigantic water tanks for transport since there is nothing on the Gili Islands but fun and sun. Gili Islands is all about the beach.

Pondok Senaru Cottages

Once in Senaru, we were "underwhelmed" by Pondok Senaru Cottages, our home for one night.The connected cottages are considered the best available. Six French, two other Americans, and two Indonesians were the lucky guests, all of whom would climb Mount Rinjani tomorrow. The **good news?** Wonderful views of Senaru Valley and Sendang Gile waterfall, dinner was good and not expensive. **The bad news (FYI only)?**

Happy Trails had said Pondok Senaru had hot water and western-style toilets. There is no hot water. What water there is barely trickled out of the sink faucet. Western style toilets? Yes, but they don't **flush;**

The cottage walls are made of woven grass; thin and not exactly soundproof. During the night, I could have sworn a man snoring in the next room was sleeping in **my** bed. It took a few "pokes" at Steve before it dawned that the world-championship snoring was coming from the next room; and

Ordering meals took unlimited patience. Requesting the majority of items listed on their menu sent us into gales of laughter. (Anything that makes me laugh can't be all bad.) For example, "I'd like toast." "So sorry, no toast." "Could I have a banana *jaffle*?" (A toasted sandwich.) "Sorry, no bread to make it with." "How about an omelet." A blank stare. Five minutes later, waiter returns, "With cheese, tomatoes?"

Sendang Gile Waterfall is easily seen from the Pondok Senaru terrace. Closer views require a 20-minute walk down a graded trail and steps from Senaru village. Follow the posted signs and return along the edge of a steep valley if you want a little variety. A second waterfall, Tiu Kelep, is an hour's walk upriver from Sendang Gile. Locals say that a swim in its deep pool will make you look a year younger. (I'd have to immerse myself for months at a time.) A walk was scheduled for closer views but neither of us felt like oozing down the mud trail.

Little did we know our afternoon walk through the forest was going to be equally squishy!

Nature Walk Through The Forests
Senaru is situated 920 meters/3,018 feet above sea level, surrounded by mountains, forest, and green, fertile fields. Happy Trails had arranged a four-hour afternoon walk led by a female guide through the forest, and rice fields, Sendang Gile Waterfall, and a traditional Sasak village. The Sasak are the cultural guardians of Mount Rinjani and its surrounding forest, and safeguard its spiritual values.

Before setting off, we asked Nasip if hiking boots were needed (brought with for this purpose), but he assured us that Tevas or sandals would be fine. Perhaps **fine** in dry conditions, **not** on uphill, slippery, and **muddy** trails.

Local guide Katni, a member of the local cooperative, arrived at 2:00p. This cooperative was established for women to earn extra money and impart knowledge about their traditional daily life, customs and nature. Katni led off, blithely (and sure-footedly) striding uphill, spewing information with every step while we slipped along behind her. She pointed out Robusto coffee beans; three kinds of bananas including one described as "banana milk"; a gigantic, poisonous spider that, believe it or not, was a "munchkin" compared to other poisonous spiders in Indonesia, Eeww...

There were spices, vanilla, and tiny green peppers that are very hot. (The smaller the pepper, the hotter it is.) Coconuts, beautiful stands of bamboo, avocado trees, and Poinsettia, referred to as the "Christmas Flower" in Lombok. Not the puny Poinsettia plants we're used to seeing around holiday season but **7-8 foot high bushes**. The Sasak people use Poinsettia as a **calendar**. All green leaves signifies the onset of the wet season and people stop planting. When flowers turn **completely red**, it is the dry season and safe to plant. Isn't that clever? The center of the large Poinsettia flower resembled mini duck heads! Hi Donald.....or, I could go into my rendition of *Rubber Duckie.*

A family was harvesting peanuts (groundnuts) in their field. Small peanuts, dug right out of the ground, have an entirely different taste, similar to a mild radish. So good, we ended up looking for these tiny, unsalted peanuts through the rest of Indonesia.

We saw hundreds of rice fields. I've written about rice fields so many times but would like to repeat what a grueling existence rice growing is. People work in the fields 12 hours a day, from 6:00a to 6:00p, 7 days a week. A terribly hard life.

The nature walk led to Rinjani National Park Trekking Center (rinjaninationalpark.com) that had trailhead signs to the crater lake.

Mount (Gunung) Rinjani Trekking Information

Senaru Village is the main gateway to Rinjani National Park, the most popular starting point for two, three, and four-day Rinjani Treks up Indonesia's second highest Peak (3,726 meters/12,224 feet). There are super-fit people who race up and down the mountain in **one day**. Don't you just hate them? The People of Lombok revere the volcano as a sacred place and abode of Gods; pilgrims go to the crater lake to place offerings in the water and bathe away disease in the nearby Hot Springs.

Rinjani National Park Trekking Center was covered with detailed maps, displays, ecotourism activities, flora and fauna, guide hire, trek options and more. Good maps and a few souvenirs were also for sale here. All trekkers **must** sign in before ascending Mount Rinjani, and **must** take a local guide. Porters can be hired from the Senaru Porters Group based in the Rinjani Trek Center. The most common trek is the 2 day/1 night trek to the crater lake from Senaru. It is **seven hours uphill** to Plawangan 1 Crater Rim Camp where visitors spent the night, watch sunset, sunrise and return the same way; another two hours from this point to Lake Camp area and Hot Springs; three more hours to Plawangan 2 Crater Rim camp; and **another** three hours to the top of Gunung Rinjani if determined to **summit**. Remember! This trek is not a piece of cake unless a seven hour walk up a mountain is easy for you.

Another trailhead begins in Sembalun. This route takes 7-1/2 hours to Plawangan 2 Crater Rim; divert from there to the Plawangan 2 Crater Rim; and then back down to Senaru or summit Mount Rinjani.

Local guide Katni belongs to the Women's Cooperative, formed 11 years ago to take visitors on walks around the area, and short treks. From here, we followed her a short distance into a Sasak Village.

A Traditional Sasak Village

This particular 300-year old Sasak Village had, perhaps, 90-99 inhabitants, all farmers. It was so quiet when we walked in that I originally thought it was **uninhabited**. Katni led us over to a fence where the Head Man was working in his rice field. Alongside the fence was a small temple with a row of stones in front, used to cook food on during rituals. This is also where sacrifices are held. The Sasak people blend their Muslim beliefs with a mixture of Hinduism and Animistic traditions even though they still consider themselves Muslim; this mixed religion is called **Wetu Telu**. The Sasak people have also developed a sensible solution to praying five times a day, as required by Islam. They have a combination "Imam/shaman" who does the **praying for them**, and the people make offerings three times a week.

A Sasak Head Man **inherits** his position. Any male family member can become the next Head Man when he dies. Head Man left the rice field, walked over to his house, and without acknowledging us, sat down, spread lime on Betel leaves, rolled and chomped away. I was interested in his old, used and abused Betel Nut box since I collect them, and discovered each person makes their own Betel Nut box. Trekkers visit the Head Man for a protection blessing before they climb Mount Rinjani.

Houses were placed in rows with additional raised platforms in the center used as extra space for overnight guests, and burial rituals. Each house was literally one big room that 10-14 family members live in; immaculately clean with every inch of space used. I suppose it would have to be neat as a pin with so many people living in one room!

Other Sasak Village facts?

- Each family had their own rice barn or granary which holds two crops of rice;

- Rice fields are passed down from generation to generation;

- Sasak people marry young; and

- When we greeted people with a "hello," **no one responded**! The Sasak don't commonly greet each other with words. They just **smile**. Ah Ha!

There are easily bookable excursions around Senaru through the Rinjani Trek Center

Ferrying From Lombok to Sumbawa Island

Just thinking about the marathon, driver and guide were going to endure over the next two days, exhausted us. They had driven **back** to Senggigi last night, returned this morning to pick us up in Senaru; we'd drive to the Labuan Lombok ferry port; take the ferry over to Sumbawa and spend two nights on the island. The drive would then continue for another **7+ hours** to **Bima** on the **other end of Sumbawa**, where driver and guide would **drop us** in Bima, and reverse the entire trip back to Lombok! What an ordeal! Nasip and Mr. Parhan would spell each other at the wheel; one sleeping, the other driving.

It was an interesting two to three-hour ride from Senaru, around the flanks of Mount Rinjani, once generic Dramamine kicked in. (Twisty, turning, and rough mountain roads guarantees a fast case of motion sickness.)

> **TIP**: Add generic Dramamine, or other motion sickness pills to your travel gear. We popped one daily on Indonesia's narrow and winding roads

Volcanic folds on mountain flanks were covered in soft, green vegetation while villagers made the most of the rich soil, working in fields of garlic, rice and corn. The drive continued east of Mount Rinjani through Sembalun Lawang, situated in an ancient, and fertile caldera. Sembalun Lawang is the preferred access route for **summiting** Rinjani. Mount Rinjani is an active volcano and seismic activity is monitored daily at the government, Rinjani Volcanology Center.

An overlook stop where monkeys came running, hoping for a handout. There was no hurry since ferries between Lombok and Sumbawa Islands leave every hour on the hour, 24 hours a day.

The road didn't become decent until we neared Labuan Lombok. Whomever prepares statistics on how often, and when ferries leave, is too optimistic. Ferries **do** run 24 hours a day, but don't count on them leaving "every hour"; Labuan Lombok does not have the fastest moving operation. We waited for **more** than an hour, looking at different foods, fruit and vegetables for sale. I even bought "Snake Fruit" remembering how tasty it was. The sun must have made me delusional, and we threw them out after one taste. Snake Fruit was **not** what I thought it was. (How could a person forget how a fruit with skin like that tasted?)

At last, the ferry disembarked passengers and smooshed on new passengers, cars, large trucks and locals who stayed on board selling items until the ferry was ready to leave. They roamed the decks with fresh chicken, soft drinks, fruit and junk food. A few people sang, hoping to earn a few Rupiah from entertaining, while a man stood with a microphone and speakers selling **toys**! Nervous, because Indonesian ferries are notorious for overloading and sinking, I was told that this was the biggest ferry between Lombok and Sumbawa Island.

THE ISLAND OF SUMBAWA

Sumbawa is a **big island**, larger than Bali and Lombok combined. Mountainous, sprawling, a coastline marked by peninsulas, inlets and coves. There are few tourists other than surfers and people like us who are crisscrossing Sumbawa. There is **nothing** to do, or see, unless surfing is your passion. The entire Lesser Sundra Island exploration was based around seeing the Komodo Dragons on Komodo and Rinca Islands. I discovered, after-the-fact, that the majority of tourists **fly** to **Labuan Bajo, Flores** first, boat to the dragon islands, end in Sape, Sumbawa, and fly from there to Lombok or Bali. The smart and easy way.

Transportation Around Sumbawa

Ferry
Ferries run from Labuan Lombok to Tano, Sumbawa 24 hours a day. Between Sape, Sumbawa to Labuan Bajo, Flores, once a day on certain days of the week (check with local operators for the most up-to-date information). There is also once a week ferry service from Sape to West Sumba.

The passage from Labuan Lombok to the port of Tano on Sumbawa Island took 1-1/2 hours, and unloaded a hell of a lot faster than it had in Lombok.

Bus
Tano is a tiny port with nothing there except buses that cross-cross the island. Public buses run from west to east through Sumbawa Besar, Bima and Sape on the East Coast, but prepare for horrible roads after Sumbawa Besar. It took us 1-1/2 hours to go **34 kilometers/21 miles**.

Crossing Sumbawa from West to East

Hotel Kencana Beach Cottages
We arrived at Kencana Beach Hotel, outside Sumbawa Besar, late in the day with numb backsides; tired, crabby, and already regretting the brainstorm to overland Sumbawa Island. Kencana had small, clean bungalows on stilts with comfortable chairs on the porch; a swimming pool; restaurant; the usual hotel perks plus Karaoke. We were the only guests tonight; thankfully, without Karaoke sessions, and it was blessedly quiet. Kencana is also situated on a beautiful stretch of deserted beach except for men fishing in the still, sunset-lit waters. Unfortunately, this gorgeous beach was missing one teensy item; **beach chairs and/or lounges**. Whine, whine, whine.

Kencana Beach Hotel advertised "hot water." There was no hot water, but at least water **flowed** out of the tap; bungalows had air conditioning that descended into the frigid realm during the night. Kencana also had a **very, very good cook**. We ate *Cumi-cumi* in garlic sauce (**squid** -- sounds obscene doesn't it), and Chicken Satay with the best, and spiciest peanut sauce we've ever eaten in Indonesia. Every cloud has a silver lining and when the silver lining is food, we're happy campers.

We scheduled two nights at Kencana Beach Hotel based on information from Happy Trails extolling the wonders of Pulau Moyo. No one tells you the **truth** about visiting Pulau Moyo (an island) but **I will**, thanks to guide Nasip. Most travel information, as well as our itinerary, stated: *"Discover moyo island... you'll have* *spectacular snorkeling here...the coral reef is still alive with some various colors, turtles is easy to see here, lot of variety of fish. You need to order box lunch and your equipment for snorkeling."*

Well! It takes two hours to get to Pulau Moyo by outrigger (a small outrigger without life jackets), and then two hours back in a rough and dangerous sea. It is a fairly deserted island, home to wild pigs, lizards, bats and monkeys. (Truthfully, all of Sumbawa was relatively deserted.) Nasip went on to say that many of his tour groups go ahead and do this optional excursion regardless of the dangers. However, **he refuses to accompany his groups and advised us not to**. We were pissed! **Do travel agents and organizers ever tell the truth?** Travels With Sheila sure does!

Eliminating Pulau Moyo left us with a rest day at Kencana, that had a deserted beach with nothing to sit on and bathtub warm water to wade in. A day spent napping, reading and girding loins for tomorrow's long ride across Sumbawa to Bima. A breakfast laugh when I requested a Banana Pancake with honey (on the menu, and one of my favorites). Pancake came without honey because, "Sorry, honey hasn't arrived from Lombok."

The Grueling Ride to Bima
I'll tell you right now. The drive from Sumbawa Besar to Bima, on the eastern end of the island, was one of the least **interesting,** and hardest, of all we've experienced. We **have** done worse and I'm not sure if that counts as bragging rights, or deserves a look of pity. A fast stop in Sumbawa Besar at a **real** mini-mart (be still my heart) to stock up on goodies, forewarned by guide Nasip that, "This was definitely it," from now on. Cookies, banana chips, two liters of water, and unsalted, little peanuts. Even Sumbawa Besar, the principal town in western Sumbawa, had no attractions worth seeing.

Today's 300 kilometer/186 mile drive to Bima would take forever on Sumbawa's main highway. Authorities have been repairing this road, using heavy machinery and workers, for over two years and construction was nowhere near being done. It was going to be a **very** long day.

Drive, drive and drive some more, for eight long hours. Occasionally, we'd hit a good stretch of road, heave a sigh of relief, thinking that was it, before more ruts and bumps. We drove past salt pans filled with water right now. Water will evaporate in a few months and locals will then harvest the salt. Overloaded buses passed each other with locals sitting on top, holding on to gigantic bags of rice and other supplies. How do they stay awake and/or keep from falling off? Car motion puts me to **sleep.**

Sumbawan people were harvesting, and drying rice and corn along the road, filling heavy bags that each weighed between **75-95 kilos/165-209 pounds,** before loading on trucks. Can you imagine carrying that kind of weight? Nasip said he could as a boy but can **only** carry **100-pound bags** now as an "older" man. (He was in his mid-30's.) Sumbawa is a very poor island that in the beginning stages of development.

More driving past fish farms, prawn (shrimp) farms, goats everywhere, horse drawn carts, motor scooters, and motor cycles. Boring, tiring, relieved only by occasional pee breaks behind trees.

A big **hallelujah** when Bima came into sight. Sumbawa was our third island visited during this trip to Indonesia with Komodo, Rinca and Flores left to go. **There is no reason to set foot on Sumbawa Island unless you have budget constraints and need to continue through the Lesser Sundra Islands**.

Bima

Almost every tourist in Bima is on their way to Rinca or Komodo Islands to see the famous Komodo dragons, exactly what we were going to do. **There are no public ferries to these islands.** Chartered boats are the only way to get there and easy to arrange through tour operators. (More about this later.) Bima is a small town, again, with nothing to see.

The La'Mbitu Hotel

Mr. Parhan pulled up in front of the tacky looking La'Mbitu Hotel, considered the best in town. Too tired to even care what the hotel looked like, the receptionist spoke English and a porter helped carry suitcases up two flights of stairs. A shower hose was held together with black plumber's tape and leaked all over the bathroom floor; the water was **hot** and the toilet **flushed**, good enough for one night. Last minute instructions for tomorrow from Nasip: breakfast at 5:30a; taxi will pick up and drive us to Sape where our chartered boat will be waiting. Fast goodbyes to Nasip and Mr. Parhan who were chomping at the bit to begin their marathon road journey back to Lombok.

With instructions from the receptionist, Steve and I set out to find an Internet place two blocks away from La'Mbitu Hotel. Happiness is a fast connection and 3,000 IDR (less than 50 cents U.S.) for one hour.

Restaurant and Hotel Lila Graha

Restaurant and Hotel Lila Graha, next to the La'Mbitu, had been recommended as the best restaurant in town by many sources. It served Indonesian food, had an English menu, and was willing to cook an early dinner for us. A Bintang beer, *gado-gado* (vegetables with peanut sauce), special fried rice and crispy noodles perked up spirits and filled stomachs with very delicious food. This entire meal cost 106,000 IDR (less than $10 U.S.) and we couldn't finish it all.

While eating, Steve noticed young students peeking in the window. They'd gather, talk among themselves, leave, peek in again until one got up his nerve to come inside and talk to the owner; local high school students, eager to practice English on the rare tourist who came through Bima. I think it showed much courage to approach total strangers who do not speak your language. We were thrilled for a chance to interact, and spent about 15 minutes, communicating back and forth, while the owner translated when they didn't quite understand what we were saying. Simple questions and answers, "Where are you from?" "**Chicago.**" Whenever we answered that question, everyone, without exception, would respond, "Obama."

The very sweet 16-17 year old teens then whipped out cell phones, and shyly asked if they could take pictures of us before leaving.

This convivial meet was the sole highlight on Sumbawa, and put smiles on our faces. A good thing because breakfast the next morning at La'Mbitu Hotel was pitiful. One scrambled egg, a cup filled with **coffee grounds** (not instant) and hot water. Fortunately, I wasn't hungry at 5:30a.

If you think I'm being **negative** about omitting Sumbawa (and I am), this is what the owner of Restaurant Lila Graha said when we asked how many westerners come through Bima. He replied, "Maybe 60 a year!" Just think; fifty-eight other dorks passed this way. That statistic will not make the Sumbawa Tourist Bureau jump for joy, will it?

Sape

A torrential downpour (what else is new) all the way through the mountains from Bima to Sape Harbor that stopped shortly before Sape. Sape is a small fishing port with ferries that run to Labuan Bajo, Flores.

Our boat, the Sea Star, was waiting at the dock. The Sea Star was bigger than anticipated and made us feel more comfortable about the sea journey; especially, after we checked out ample life jackets and radio communications. The Sea Star sleeps at least **18 people** in one long room with bunks separated by a curtain. It had air conditioning and fan in the sleeping area, a toilet on the shaded main deck, and the upper deck had padded lounge chairs. This, was all **ours**! Captain and a crew of four were ready to make the journey comfortable. The last time we had a boat to ourselves was in Borneo, visiting the Orangutans. (What a fabulous trip that was!) None of our crew spoke more than a few words of English, but somehow we managed to communicate. It would have been helpful if Happy Trails had given more in-depth information on **exactly** what the two days included since I'm sure there were many *lost in translation* moments.

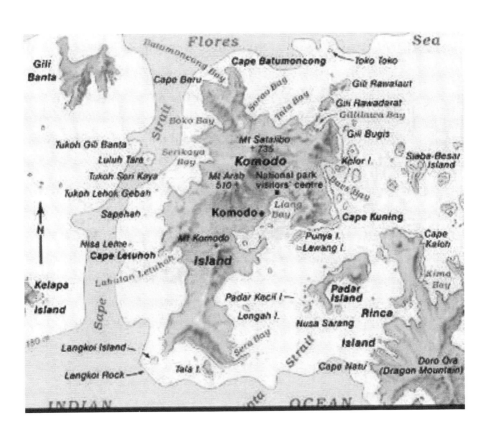

KOMODO AND RINCA ISLAND NATIONAL PARKS

Komodo National Park includes three major islands: Komodo, Rinca, Padar, and numerous smaller islands. Both Komodo and Rinca are hilly and desolate islands, sandwiched between Flores and Sumbawa; **the only place in the world where one can see the legendary Komodo dragons, the world's largest lizard.** It is a UNESCO World Heritage Site and you **must** have a local guide (ranger) accompany you (unless you have a death wish) while trekking on both Komodo and Rinca; guides are available on both islands. It cost 50,000 IDR ($5.00 U.S.) for a ranger, conservation fee of $15.00 U.S./person, entrance fees and camera fees, for a total of $25 U.S. per person a day.

Komodo Dragon Facts

The Komodo Dragon is the biggest reptile on the planet and closely related to the dinosaurs. However, it is **not** a dinosaur but the **world's largest lizard**;

A female lays an average of 35 eggs that she buries in deep mounds. Eight months later, the youngsters run up the nearest tree they see to avoid getting eaten. The young live in trees hunting for insects, rodents and birds until it becomes too heavy. On the ground, it begins eating wild pigs, deer, horses and buffaloes. An occasional human is also tasty if they come across one;

These dominant predators rely on camouflage and patience, waiting for passing prey. Komodo Dragons **eviscerate** their victims. Even those lucky enough to escape will soon die of blood poisoning; their saliva is filled with over **50 strains of bacteria.** Yuck--ee.... Dragons will follow an escapee for miles until the animal drops dead;

Komodo Dragons eat 50 kilos/110 pounds in a single feeding, and then fast for one month. (I would make a good meal, however, Steve would make a better one);

Their long forked tongue gives it a keen sense of smell. They can seek out prey from up to **8 kilometers/ 5 miles away** in a favorable wind. Their tongues test the air, taste, and smell;

Komodo Dragons can run as fast as **20 kilometers/12.3 miles an hour** in brief sprints; and

There are approximately 3,000-5,000 Komodo Dragons on the islands of Komodo, Gila Motang, Rinca, and Flores. Komodo and Rinca are the **only** islands tourists are allowed to visit. This species is considered **endangered.**

How to get to Komodo National Park?

Think, not easy; **Boat is the only option.** There are no public ferries currently operating between Sumbawa and Flores that stop at either Komodo Island or Rinca Island. Rinca receives a few more visitors than Komodo because it's nearer to the port of Labuan Bajo in Flores; the main jumping-off point for trips to Komodo

National Park. I recommend chartering a boat from there rather than Sape unless you use a reputable tour operator, e.g. Happy Trails; Sape has a reputation for not very seaworthy boats.

You can even do a day trip to Rinca. Your boat will leave Labuan Bajo around 8:00a, sail for two hours to Rinca, and then return by way of snorkeling spots. The boats hold up to 10 passengers. A day-trip to Komodo Island takes four hours each way, harder to do in one day but still doable. Another option is to take a seven-day cruise from Bali that stops at these islands.

> TIP: Whatever you do, **make sure your boat has a radio and lifejackets**! These isolated islands are surrounded by some of the worst seas in Indonesia with rip-tides, whirlpools and horrendous storms.

This information is **deadly serious**. A Bali-based Perama tour boat went down March 28, 2011 near Komodo Island during a big storm; 17 tourists were aboard along with eight crew. Everyone did survive reporting that, "**Most of the lifejackets could not be used**. They were knotted, tied together and stuck underneath a mesh cloth that was difficult to open," and the **vessel's lifeboat was not operational**. Let's talk shades of Titanic minus an ice berg.

A chance to experience a **private** chartered boat ride through the Komodo archipelago is considered to be a highlight by most tourists. Steve and I would spend one night on board the boat and have all the bunk beds to ourselves; a cook would prepare meals; there **were** plentiful life jackets onboard and a **radio**. Captain always coordinated with the harbor officer for permission to boat. If the harbor officer said weather was bad, the trip would be postponed. **That** would be a bummer since this trip was arranged to visit the Komodo Dragons in its natural habitat.

We chose April, even though it was still rainy season, based on advice from Happy Trails. Dragons usually mate in May and disappear into the bushes, making them harder to locate. (They like to do their mating in private.)

Boating to Komodo Island

Praying for good weather, and non-mating Komodo dragons, the crew raised anchor and we sailed off on a seven-hour ride to Komodo Island with views of Tambora Volcano. Tambora's peak was **obliterated** in 1815 during one of the greatest volcanic explosions of modern times. It has been quiet since then and can be climbed on a hard, two-day trip.

Komodo Island came into view two hours later, but it is a big island and took a long time to make our way around the island to Komodo National Park. Steve and I spent the day racing to from side to side whenever the crew shouted, "Dolphins"; dozed on the top deck and comfortable, padded long seats in the shade when the sun became too hot; drank coffee and munched on cookies/biscuits. A yummy lunch at noon: rice, fried shrimp, spicy noodles, vegetable stir fry, and bananas for dessert; I could easily get used to living like this.

Komodo Dragons on Komodo Island

Let it be said right from the get-go. There is **never** a guarantee you'll spot a Komodo Dragon in the **wild** but there are usually a few hanging around the kitchens on both islands. The Park Service on Komodo Island feeds the dragons in the morning; chicken and fish. They used to throw the odd goat or two in the past to keep tourists from being disappointed if they didn't see one lurking in the underbrush. I don't think a chicken or fish would go far in sating a Komodo Dragon's intake of 50 kilos/110 pounds at one sitting. That would take many chickens.

The Sea Star moored close to the Loh Liang jetty on Komodo Island around 3:00p. Captain dropped anchor and we were assisted into a little dinghy towed behind the boat. Neither of us understood why we had to take a dinghy when a long pier was available with no other boats tied up. Ah...little grasshopper, the ways of others are beyond me. It was just us and the Komodo Dragons this afternoon since the majority of tourists work their way west from Flores to Rinca to Komodo Island. Komodo Island is the largest of the islands in the Komodo National Park (komodonationalpark.org).

A member of the crew accompanied us to the main office for check-in; carrying paperwork since we had prepaid entrance, camera and guide fees. There are hiking trails throughout the National Park but it **is not permitted to walk without a guide** as dragons have occasionally attacked, and killed, humans. There are small fishing villages on Komodo Island and locals are periodically dragged off and eaten; rare but it does happen. Guide Latif asked us to stay together and not wander off. Was he crazy? Wander off? Steve and I made one silhouette. Latif armed himself with the traditional forked stick to keep away dragons, selected the Forest Trail and off we went, sticking to him like glue, towards a water hole. Perhaps, a Komodo Dragon would be lurking in the underbrush waiting for a deer.

There are four different treks to choose from: Easy takes one hour; Medium 1-1/2 hours; hard and adventurous 2+ hours. Even if you pick the hardest trek, there is **still** no guarantee that you'll see one of the 1,200 dragons on Komodo Island. One hour, one and a half hours sounds very easy until you experience the steam heat on Komodo Island; sweat poured off with each step. Those of you who have grown up in a Houston, Texas summer will have no problem.

We squished through the mud and saw...an oriole...a pigeon. Continued on and saw...palm trees. More walking. A wild pig disappeared into the bush. Still walking, Latif tried to keep up our interest level by talking about palm trees since there was nothing interesting to see. **Nirvana.** Towards the end of this boring forest walk, Latif spotted a baby Komodo Dragon high in the crack of a cave; how he saw it, I'll never know. The baby was perhaps two months old and would stay concealed in the rock crack for another month. Older dragons eat the babies if they are on the ground.

Fortunately, four Komodo Dragons **were** hanging around the kitchen area - an adult male and a few younger ones. Latif kept urging me to get closer for photographs. (The shaky video attests to the fact that I was **not** getting **closer** and telephoto'd in the best I could.) **Please visit travelswithsheila channel on YouTube.com to watch all the videos.**

The unexpected baby Komodo Dragon sighting was thrilling but this experience was not as stupefying as envisioned. However, we can now add it to our "been there...done it" list. Back past a gauntlet of men selling pearls and carved Komodo dragons to the Sea Star. Coffee and snarfing down yummy, but strange saltine crackers that were sweet as well as salty, we motored off towards Rinca Island where the Captain would moor for the night along the beautiful coastline.

We'd visit the dragons on Rinca Island tomorrow. For now, more rain, dinner and sleep. Or, try to sleep. The Sea Star left lights on throughout the night. Try sleeping with a light bulb hanging over your head, and a noisy generator. Add in climbing up and down ladders to the bathroom, and trying not to fall on rain slick decks. I finally dug out the old ear plugs, covered eyes with a towel and dozed off.

Komodo Dragons of Rinca Island

Rinca is the second biggest island of Komodo National Park, closer to Labuan Bajo in Flores, and the landscape is greener and hillier than that of Komodo.

The same routine, information and fees apply for both islands; guides, conservation fee, entrance fee, camera fees. There are no set dragon-feeding places on Rinca and finding dragons in the bush isn't easy. Guides know the favorite spots, dragon nests (females dig huge burrows to lay their eggs which they guard until they hatch), and whatever wildlife is around. Dragons also inhabit Pulau Padar and coastal areas of northwestern **Flores**; I've never heard of anyone going to these places.

The crew served breakfast early in the morning, Captain weighed anchor and motored a short distance away to the dock at Rinca. No dinghy today, and only one other boat was tied to the dock. Good deal!

A member of the crew accompanied us again on a five-minute walk from the dock to the Rinca National Park Office for formalities. Today's Komodo Dragon number one was sitting under a tree along the way; so still that I thought it was a **carved Komodo dragon** put there to greet visitors. We stood around and waited with another couple from Toronto, Canada until officials arrived to open the office and assign guides. Both Komodo and Rinca have PHKA camps. The camps have large wooden cabins on stilts with balconies, restaurants; only one-night stays allowed.

Rinca rangers **do not** feed the dragons who come out of the forest when they smell food. The Komodo Dragon's long forked tongue gives it a keen sense of smell. They can seek out prey from up to **8 kilometers/5 miles away** in a favorable wind. Their tongues test the air, taste, and smell. Komodo Dragons are solitary, coming together only to breed and eat. Lured by odors from the kitchen, **six** Komodo were sitting in the kitchen area this morning. New guide Armand said they'd lurk here for most of the day before heading back into the forest to hunt.

Armand grabbed his forked stick of choice (they use the forked end to push the dragon's head away), went through the usual welcome spiel, and the three of us headed out on the "moderate" walk, taken during rainy season, with a brief stop at the bathrooms first. Steve almost had heart failure when he walked out of the bathroom, and saw another Komodo sitting there. Komodo can run as fast as **20 kilometers/12.3 miles an hour** in brief sprints, a lot faster than us, and he had a right to be frightened. They are scary looking critters with powerful hind quarters and nasty claws.

The trail was muddy, and revealed nothing but one or two dragon nests. Mating begins between May and August, and approximately 20 eggs are laid in big nesting holes in September. The eggs incubate for seven to eight months, and hatch in April (when we were here). No baby Komodo today, Armand said they are usually seen in trees on sunny afternoons.

It is difficult to spot Komodo during the rainy season because foliage is so high. We slogged back to the main camp where a seventh dragon had joined the other six by the kitchen, and posed for photographs a safe distance away. Armand kept saying, "Get closer. Go ahead, get closer." No way, Armand. Not with several dragons flicking that long tongue out, sensing prey (us), and looking in our direction.

Armand came with us for the walk back to the boat, past the same Komodo "greeter" still sitting under its tree, and then spotted another Komodo Dragon, perfectly concealed in brush next to the trail. We count "him" as our only "wild dragon" sighting since all the others were out in the open, giving us a total of **10 Komodo Dragons** today. With 1,300 dragons on Rinca Island, there were still plenty left to see. One hundred people visited Rinca Island yesterday, and several boats were heading in with more tourists as we motored out on the way to Labuan Bajo, Flores. Bye, bye, dragons.

It was an uneventful two-hour cruise from Rinca Island to Labuan Bajo on Flores Island which gave us time to gather up belongings spread all over the unused bunks. A few dolphin/porpoise sightings (I can't tell the difference), fishing and dive boats also making their way towards Labuan Bajo Harbor.

Thanks and tips to the wonderful crew who were always feeding us cookies/biscuits, and into a car up to Golo Hilltop Hotel for one night. **Hello, Flores**.

Flores island

INTENSELY GREEN, MOUNTAINOUS & VOLCANIC FLORES ISLAND

Flores is one of the Lesser Sundra Islands and our last island on this visit. A green, mountainous island created by a chain of volcanic cones stretching its length. Because of Flores' topography, there is only one "good" road crossing the island; the Trans-Flores highway. The road winding through the mountains is in **decent** shape (relatively better than Sumbawa), but **slow**. Twenty-five ton trucks routinely ply this Trans-Flores highway on a road meant to be used by vehicular traffic weighing less than **seven tons**.

Population is estimated around 1.5 million, divided into five main linguistic and cultural groups. Most tourists see only Labuan Bajo on the West coast and Maumere, Flores' largest town unless making their way from island to island, or across the island. Maumere would be our final destination in Flores before flying back to Bali.

Transportation

Air
IAT, Merpati Airlines, TransNusa, Wings Air (Lionair), and Batavia Air fly to/from Denpasar from Labuan Bajo, Maumere and Ende. Almost all intra-Indonesia flights make more than one stop on their routes. Schedules are irregular; some airlines offer once a day flights while others fly only certain days a week. There is a departure tax of 10,000 IDR ($1.00 U.S.)

Bus, Bemo and Trucks
Independent travelers can easily make their way from one end of Flores to the other using any one of these combinations.

Ferries and Boats
The **easiest** way to visit the **Komodo Dragon Islands** is to: fly into Labuan Bajo, Flores; hire a private boat or book group travel through one of the tour operators to the dragon islands; fly from Sumbawa to Lombok or Bali.

Different boats sail from Labuan Bajo, Maumere, Ende, and Larantuka to: Makassar, Sulawesi; Kalimantan; Kupang, Timor; Surabaya; and Sumba. Ask a local tour operator for up-to-date information.

Flores Information and Trivia

Flores is a poor island. Only people who work for the Government, Civil Service and Chinese businessmen do well. The rest of the people survive on anywhere from 7-10 million IDR's ($700-1,000 U.S.) a year;

People live simply raising rice, corn, taro, cucumbers, vegetables, bananas, and coconuts in rich soil, due to its volcanoes. Only 20% of Flores is able to be cultivated and every inch is used;

There are world class diving sites along the North coast of Flores and around Labuan Bajo. We saw beautiful, live-aboard dive boats in both Labuan Bajo Harbor and the Flores Sea;

Flores is almost entirely Roman Catholic, **unusual in Indonesia, the world's most populous Muslim-majority country.** Catholicism was introduced by the Portuguese who came in 1512, and stayed until the seventeenth century when the Dutch kicked them out;

"Labuan" means harbor. That explains why there is a "Labuan Lombok", "Labuan Bajo" Flores, etc.

Kelimutu Volcano, near Moni, contains three colored lakes in its caldera; the lakes change color depending on the current state of oxidation;

Ruteng, in the heart of Manggarai (an ethnic group) country, is surrounded by the famous "spider" rice fields;

The mountainsides around Bajawa are studded with small and traditional Ngada villages; and

Flores guide Ricardos referred to us as Ibu Sheila and Pak Steve, a term showing respect to elders.

WHAT TO SEE AND DO ON FLORES ISLAND

Labuan Bajo

Labuan Bajo is a small fishing community that attracts divers, snorkelers and people heading to the Komodo Islands. A small airport is close to town and several companies operate flights in and out of Labuan Bajo airport: Indonesia Air Transport (IAT), TransNusa, Merpati Airlines, Wings Air and Batavia Air. Buses to Ruteng, Bajawa and Ende operate on certain days of the week.

In town, you'll find: Internet, ATMs, banks, restaurants, guesthouses and many tour operators.

Golo Hilltop Hotel
A car from Golo Hilltop Hotel (golohilltop.com) came to the harbor and transferred us up the mountain. Golo Hilltop Hotel is situated on top of a hill (duh...), about 1 kilometer/.6 mile from the city center, in a quiet, relaxing location. All rooms are in long bungalows on different hill levels with a sitting area outside each room. The bungalows have **either:** fans or air conditioning, hot or cold water, depending on your budget; we opted for hot water and air conditioning. Golo Hilltop is Dutch run with a restaurant that served "average-tasting" food. However, the restaurant was open, airy and had beautiful views of the bay, little islands and dive boats making their way across the sea. Quite a few guests used Golo Hilltop as a **base**, to spend days diving in different locations. Whale sharks inhabit the waters in this area.

We were very confused about our Flores plans going forward since neither the hotel, nor us, knew anything about who, what and where.

> **TIP: Always carry the local telephone number of your tour operator for emergencies**.

Golo Hilltop called the tour agency, who told them new driver and guide would pick us up tomorrow morning at 8:00a to begin our Flores Island exploration.

Steve and I considered walking down to the center of town until it began raining heavily, **again**. Kill me if I ever, ever arrange to travel during rainy season!

Spider Web Rice Terraces of Lodok Cara

Each day held new surprises since the Happy Trails itinerary only had sketchy details. Flores guide Ricardos and driver Nikolas pulled off the road to Ruteng, and stopped in front of a small house that said, Lodok Cara Village. I asked, "What are we doing here?" "Going to see a view of rice fields." "Where?" Ricardos pointed uphill. Confused, we followed him into a dark house where he told us to give village Head Man a small donation, and sign names in a register. Formalities over, we walked back outside with Ricardos, Head Man following.

Taking walking sticks, we began climbing mud steps on a the hillside path to a viewpoint; hanging on to bamboo railings and through vegetation. And what a viewpoint it was! Looking down, and as far as the eye could see, were **concentric rice fields that resembled gigantic spider webs**. These fields were built by the Manggarai people. The Manggarai have a political system built on clans; each clan gets a piece of the land called *Lodok* by the local people. The field wedges looked **unequal** but looks were deceiving, as explained by Ricardos...

"Each person in the clan is given a fair share. When they have a son, a piece of the pie is divided and given to that son. If you have four more sons, four more pieces are cut off and given to that son." Their houses are built with a conical roof **mirroring** the fields.

Not only was the viewpoint unusual, but the first time we've ever seen rice fields **shaped like spider webs**. Next stop? A typical Manggarai Village, Golo Ceru, and we hustled off because it looked like **rain** again.

Golo Ceru
Golo Ceru had only two houses **rebuilt** in typical Manggarai style with one difference; the original version wouldn't have had any **windows**. I sent Steve in to make donation and sign guest book while I waited outside hoping there would be something more than two houses to see. There was. A circle in the center held a Banyan tree (believed to be spiritual); monolithic rock used for ceremonies, rituals, dancing, sacrifices; and graves of important villagers. I can't tell you how long it took me to understand that the vaunted "**monolithic rock**" was this **circle**. *A monolith is a geological feature such as a mountain, consisting of a single massive stone or rock, or a single piece of rock.* Okey-dokey...

Traditional houses were once conical and arranged in concentric circles **around** the round, sacrificial arena. Nothing old remained; everything had been destroyed and modern houses built. One of the rebuilt houses was called the "Drum House" and **would** have housed drums, Gamelons, other musical instruments and heirlooms. The other house belonged to the chief and was divided inside for the different village clans. I referred to it as a "Manggarai conference room" since each clan would send a representative here for important meetings. Clan reps would then go back to their villages with big news, "Hey, we are going to have a ………. Ceremony over at the Chief's house. Liquor, dancing, a good sacrifice, and gossip. Let's **Par-tee**."

The spider web rice fields were **outstanding**, the village **underwhelming**; let's move on to Ruteng.

Hill Town of Ruteng

Ruteng was the first large town near Labuan Bajo and only140 kilometers/87 miles away. By now, it was 2:30p, and we were **starving**. Ricardos took us to **Agape Cafe** in Ruteng (pronounced Rucheng). Recommended by other guide books, it was the only place his agency considered suitable for western stomachs. Good *Lumpini/ Lumpia* (egg rolls), and so-so bland noodles that tasted better when we added chili sauce. Ruteng had two other recommended restaurants, but Ricardos had his instructions; Agape Cafe it had to be with no deviations.

Ruteng is a cool, clean city surrounded by volcanic hills and rice fields. Most tourists stay for one night only before heading back on the road; exactly what we would do. The **only** interesting sight in Ruteng is its market, a central meeting point for the local Manggarai people. The Manggarai weave, and wear, a typical sarong that I was only interested in **seeing**, not buying.

The Ruteng market was deserted because it was Easter weekend. All supermarkets (mini-marts) in Ruteng were closed and would remain closed, tomorrow, Easter Sunday. The market was heavy on stinky, smelly, dried fish. Only one stall sold typical Manggarai sarongs that looked like an optical illusion when you looked at them dead on. Other than schmoozing with whatever friendly salespeople happened to be sitting around, there was **nothing** to do in Ruteng. We walked out of the market, the usual afternoon rain began; fortunately, we had finished seeing all that Ruteng had to offer.

Susteran Bunda Maria Hotel

A mad dash into the car for a ride over to our hotel, Susteran Bunda Maria Hotel. We had no idea where we were staying or where it was located, since Happy Trails had changed hotels on us. Not a bad thing since Susteran Bunda Maria Hotel was considered the best available in Ruteng. Part of a **monastery** located east of Ruteng, the "hotel" section is a convent with 30 nuns and many novices. This two-story building had 20 rooms with bathrooms, hot and cold running water, no restaurant. They do serve a small breakfast, included in the rate. Rooms were on the small size with a double bed that had one side smack up against one wall. Guess who would have to climb over the other to use the bathroom?

Not at all hungry for dinner since we had just finished lunch, we asked Ricardos if he could rustle up some bread to make tuna sandwiches. He asked one of the sisters, and she turned up at **9:00p** carrying a plate of bread. Umm...not hungry now, but thanks

> **TIP**: Foil, easy-to-open pouches of tuna salad go everywhere with us. Great for emergencies, like now!

The breakfast room at Susteran Bunda Maria Hotel was **"filled"** on a sunny, Easter Sunday; two Danes and an American from San Francisco were sitting there, traveling in the opposite direction towards Labuan Bajo by using public transportation. According to the Danes, the best diving in Flores is around Labuan Bajo - better than Sulawesi and even better than the Philippines. The three also agreed that this little hotel run by the monastery was a miraculous find compared to dirty, bug-laden dumps they usually stayed in for the same price; **15,000 Rupiah a night (less than $2.00 U.S.) including breakfast**.

Breakfast was on the skimpy side. One fried egg, rice, two pieces of toast and coffee but what do you expect for **$2.00 U.S. a night**? Too bad they didn't kill that damn rooster crowing from 4:00a on, and serve **it** for breakfast!

Bajawa

Bajawa, with Ngada traditional villages in the area, is supposed to be a Flores highlight. The six-hour drive began on a narrow road that didn't stop winding or turning, the entire way. Stops for pee breaks along the road in the forest (hunker down, do your "business"; keep a sharp eye out for snakes; look at unusual vegetation; return to vehicle). Stop to look at an uninspiring lake from a viewpoint. Another stop in a small town to replenish our cookie, peanut stash, led to a cheese cracker discovery that was so yummy, we promptly snarfed down half the box.

Past a local church with people gathered outside for Easter Sunday services. When I asked Ricardos to stop to see what was going on, children came running from all directions. Because few Westerners come through Flores, children get excited when they spot tourist vehicles zooming along the road (tour company names are plastered on the sides). And they practically go into **orbit** if a tourist takes time to **stop** and **talk**.

Today was the children's lucky day as I, unintentionally, disrupted the church service. (Sorry, didn't mean to.) One little boy knew enough English to ask, "What is your name?" while others called out **"Hello Mister"** as they ran down the hill towards me. Guide Ricardos said that people on Flores use three words to describe Westerners: "**Tourist**"; "**Bulay**" = albino or white person; and "**Mister**" whether a person is male or female. Now I knew why people were always shouting "Hello Mister" at me.

One, last interesting stop before Bajawa; to see how *Arak* is made. What is *Arak*? Think...40-45% alcohol content, 100+ proof firewater!

How to Make Arak (potent firewater)
What is Arak? Arak is a highly alcoholic spirit and traditional home-brewed drink in Indonesia. Think of: stills, firewater, hootch, moonshine, red-eye, rotgut, and you've got the idea. Imported alcohol can be taxed **400%** in Indonesia so locals brew their own. Chances are you'll be offered a drink of Arak somewhere in Indonesia. I strongly suggest to take a pass unless you are 100% positive your glass of Arak was brewed safely, and carefully. Four foreigners **died of alcohol poisoning** in July 2009, a few days after our Java/Bali trip. At last count, 23 tourists have died in Bali and Lombok from Arak while other foreigners and locals have been taken ill. Victims drank Arak tainted with **methanol**, known as wood alcohol, and used in rural Indonesia as **fuel for lanterns.**

It is illegal to sell alcohol without a license in Indonesia but according to Ricardos, the government looks the other way because it is part of the culture. No important event, ritual or ceremony takes place without Arak. Different varieties of Arak are distilled from grapes, anise, grain, molasses, plums, figs and potatoes in other parts of the world. You may know also these libations as: Ouzo, Raki, Mastika, and in Iran, "Dog's sweat!"

Stands began appearing along one particular stretch of road displaying filled water bottles. Indonesians used old water bottles to hold and sell everything. They obviously weren't filled with gasoline/petrol (a deep yellow color that looks like urine), soft drinks or distilled water. The liter bottles were filled with Arak, made from the male fruit of a particular palm tree. The finished alcohol content ranges from 40-45% and more than 100 proof. Enough to knock the strongest person flat on their back if they don't go blind first.

Men climb a particular species of palm that bears male fruit, and squish the fruit daily while still on the palm tree for five days. (Squishing male fruit daily sounds obscene but that's exactly what they do.)

The fruit's liquid drips into a bucket high on the palm tree.

The Arak makers climb the palm on the sixth day to get the juice bucket which is then distilled over a wood fire.

The clear liquid drips through a bamboo pipe into a 1-liter or 2-liter water bottle.

The first dripping of Arak is the most powerful while the second and third proofs are **only** 20% alcohol and 15% alcohol, respectively; still enough to get a good buzz going. Ricardos insisted on igniting some Arak for us to see how strong it was. (I bet pouring Arak, instead of kerosene, around a dwelling could set off quite a conflagration.) The owner then offered samples of his **strongest** distillation, 50-63% alcohol content, 100+ proof firewater! Even though his Arak was supposed to be very pure, we nicely refused.

A liter bottle of the first dripping cost 100,000 IDR ($10 U.S.); 45,000 IDRs for a smaller bottle (less than $5 U.S.). Now that you know what we know about **Arak**, drink at your own risk.

Views of the sea, volcanos, and the hill town of Bajawa, situated at 1,200 meters/3,600 feet above sea level was in sight. This Ngada district is one of the most traditional areas in Flores. Tomorrow, we'd visit Luba and Bena, two megalithic villages.

Bintang Wisata Hotel, Bajawa
Our small hotel for two nights was Bintang Wisata, located in the heart of Bajawa next to the market, shopping areas and restaurants. This hotel was adequate, filled with tourists, had spacious rooms with attached bathrooms, and hot water. Another sparse breakfast at the Hotel Bintang Wisata. (We'd lose weight if it wasn't for all the junk food runs into mini-marts to supplement our diet.)

Recommended Restaurants
We ate lunch at **Lucus**, one of the three restaurants that cater to tourists; the other two are: Camellia and Ditos. Lucas was the only game in town on Easter Sunday, and we settled in for noodles, rice and chicken *satay* while rain thundered down on the tin roof so loud, it was impossible to hear, or talk over it. Eating lunch at 3:30p has one advantage: think of it as combo lunch and dinner to extend your budget.

There was plenty of time to Internet back in Bajawa on a good connection at Warnet, followed by an early lunch/diner at Camellia's. Our motto? Stick to what is filling and what they do best in the Lesser Sundra Islands. With all the noodles and rice we've eaten throughout Indonesia, our bodies probably are sufficiently carbo loaded to finish an ultra marathon.

Ngada Volcanos and Villages in Flores

The best part of arranging a private trip, or traveling independently, is the ability to change your itinerary; exactly what we did. Guide Ricardos constantly offered to stop the car throughout Flores at different overlooks and viewpoints, repeating, "Tourists come to Flores for the mountain scenery." Sorry, but how many mountain visuals can a person take before overload is followed by boredom? We now know why the Lesser Sundra Islands is "the road not often taken by tourists." Omitting local meets that we loved, Flores was boring. Our poor tour guide was appalled when we decided to cut the trip short, if feasible and skip Soa Hot Springs and Riung, a beach stop for snorkeling. With that, Ricardos grabbed his cell/mobile phone and went to work changing the flight out of Maumere to Denpasar along with all hotel reservations. A done deal.

In the car for a one-hour ride into the mountains surrounding Bajawa and past Inerie Volcano to a viewpoint. Volcanos everywhere, different Ngada villages with thatch roofs tucked in the mountainsides, and the blue Sawu sea in the distance. Nage, Wogo, Langa, Bela, Luba and Bena are the most commonly visited villages; a few are more modern than others.

The Ngada people belong to clans and marriages take place strictly inside their own clan. Cousins are allowed to marry, land is portioned out to clan members, and the oldest child receives the family inheritance.

Our driver let us out along a main road leading up to Luba Village and drove away to park at Bena Village, the most visited Ngada village in the region. On the walk to Luba Village, Ricardos related information about life in this area. We looked at: mangos, papaya, avocados and cacao (where chocolate comes from). People were cutting, and carrying, wild taro to feed their pigs, and collected Candlenuts collected off the ground. Candlenut is a flowering tree common in Indonesia. Nuts turn yellow before dropping off, villagers collect the nuts, dry, and use the seeds inside with their high oil content to cook with. Parts of the plant are also used in traditional medicines, e.g. Candlenut oil is an **irritant** and can be used like castor oil.

We saw another variety of palm tree used by the locals to make **Arak**. These gigantic, and pendulous, clusters of small fruits are **cut off first** before squeezing for several weeks to get the palm juice out, and distilling.

Luba Traditional Ngada Village
Luba Village (pop: 200 people) was small, quiet, and had just a few villagers sitting around. Ricardos referred to them as of, "Ladanese" ethnicity, but even by diligent Internet surfing, and spelling "Ladanese" differently, I couldn't come up with any information. Ngada villages are composed of wooden pile houses with thatch roofs that surround a main square. Your clan determines its status in the pecking order. We entered Luba, registered, paid a 10,000 IDR donation and Ricardos got sidetracked by a man making machetes. A long discussion with him until Ricardos placed an order for a machete that will be hung in his house to **ward off evil spirits**. I guess Machetes serve more than one function in Flores. Meanwhile, machete maker's **90-year old mother** sat in the shade sorting through her stash of betel nuts in preparation for a fast chew.

The Ngada are Roman Catholic, but still cling to animist beliefs: ancestor worship and sacrifice. Family members are buried next to their houses with an occasional bottle of **Arak** and other libations placed on the graves.

Many of the thatch roofs had unusual decorations on top; spears for protection, effigies, and small house replicas. Each had a meaning and was displayed on roofs of the most important clan members. I remember seeing a witch doctor's house in West Africa with an effigy on top that, **supposedly**, could **see** visitors coming, and warn the witch doctor.

Houses were decorated with buffalo horns and pig jawbones, showing the family's prosperity (similar to Torajaland in Sulawesi). Luba had four male ancestor parasols (*ngadhus)* in the center square. I'll refer to them as "totems" for ease. Each belonged to a specific clan and had different rituals associated with them. Before a male totem is built, a baby pig or dog is sacrificed and buried in this spot. The totem is completed and big stones piled around the main post; representing this clan's generations, male and female descendants. A water buffalo, a symbol of fertility, is then tied between the male ancestor symbol and a wall; its throat cut in a way that blood spatters on the totem; and the ceremony is over. Time to dance, drink Arak and celebrate.

There were also three, female ancestor houses (*bhagas)* opposite the male ancestor houses that resembled small rice granaries. Unlike the male totems, Female ancestor houses are only built when **someone has a vision**. The fourth *bhaga* had fallen apart, and until someone in the clan has a **vision**, it will not be rebuilt.

Bena Traditional Ngada Village
A road led from Luba Village down to Bena (pop: 300) where our driver sat waiting. Bena had 16 houses lined up on both sides of a rectangle containing a stone altar, *ngadhus* and *bhagas* worshipping houses. Signed the register, made a donation and began walking around the rectangle. Bena women sat on porches, sorting rice, weaving Ikat sarongs and scarfs that were then hung on a bamboo pole to sell. A double take when I spotted one woman with what looked like blood around her mouth, and then she held up a Betel nut to show me what she was doing; just chewing away.

We continued along, admiring the roofs in this beautiful, little village. Bena is one of the most traditional Ngada villages on the flanks of Inerie Volcano, and its stone monuments are a protected site. There are stone steps leading to the center stone altar at the highest point, above the male and female ancestor clan totems. Before the Dutch missionaries came, the Ngada worshipped a male high god and his female counterpart. Sacrifices (usually a buffalo) still take place on the megalithic stones in front of the high altar, and then the *ngadhus/ bhagas* are smeared with blood.

Since Ricardos had already given important explanations about Ngada rituals and way of life, we didn't spend as much time in Bena as we had in Luba. Took more photographs, chatted up whatever locals that weren't working in the fields, and began the car journey back to Bajawa.

Volcano Climbs and Trekking in Flores

I'm sure you know Indonesia is located in the Pacific Ring of Fire. This **Ring of Fire** stretches for **40,000 kilometers/25,000 miles** in a horseshoe shape, and is associated with volcanic belts and tectonic plate movements under the earth's crust. The Ring of Fire has 452 volcanoes and is home to over **75% of the world's active and dormant volcanoes.**

Indonesia has 130 active volcanos, more than any other country in the world, and the rugged Flores landscape is full of active, and extinct, volcanoes. The Lesser Sundra Islands have 22-24 volcanoes (depends who you listen to).

Inerie Volcano

Inerie last erupted in 1882 and 1905; a perfect cone towering in the sky at a height of 2,245 meters/7,365 feet. It's easy to schedule a climb of Inerie Volcano beginning from Watu Meze village on the North side near Bajawa, or Watu Village on the South side; a climb of approximately 10 hours roundtrip if you begin on the North side. Ricardos pointed out different volcanos during the ride through Flores with the great majority, climbable and difficult.

Mount Ebulobo

Flores' most active volcano is **Mount Ebulobo** ("Grand Father Mountain"). Ebulobo is a stratovolcano (*a large, steep volcano built up of alternating layers of lava and ash or cinders*), and always smoking. This volcano has eight former eruption sites and three lava plugs. (Steve and I had a great experience hiking up Mount Bromo in Java two years ago.)

It is possible to hire a guide and climb Mount Ebulobo from Boawae. This usually calls for an overnight on the mountain followed by a two-hour, early morning climb to the summit. Again, Ricardos has been there, done it with many different groups. Boawae also has unusual boxing rituals from May to August during harvest festivities. Men put on gloves studded with **broken glass**...eeww... Don't want to see that but did enjoy standing along the road, watching Ebulobo belch smoke.

Trekking

Tourists are able to visit many of the more difficult to access Ngada Villages in the Bajawa area by long treks from jump-off points.

Blue Stones on The Way to Moni

Still heading east on the Trans-Flores Highway, we passed small communities harvesting rice fields. The entire village will pitch in to harvest one field after another. An interesting form of transport for remote villages in this area was big, open sided trucks.

A blue stone beach was next on the road towards Ende. I noticed sacks of blue stones along the highway, and people walking on the beach collecting them. These were **natural blue stones**; some in the lightest shades of turquoise while others were a little darker, and only found along this particular section of the Flores coast. Locals collect and sell for export to use in buildings, and as building material. I was chomping at the bit to get out of the car and load up a bag with these beauties, but no sooner had the driver parked, and my feet hit the sand then the skies opened up. I scooped up one handful and dashed back into the car, mourning over blue stones left behind all the way to Ende. Steve was secretly thrilled, envisioning a suitcase filled with **rocks**.

Lunch at Mentari Hotel & Restaurant in Ende with only enough time to slurp down a fast dish of fried rice before continuing to Moni. Ricardos stopped in front of a restaurant in Moni to show a sign with pictures of a pig and dog. Sign like this show people exactly what is being served inside; pig and **dog**.

The rain didn't stop until we drew closer to Moni, the jumping off point to see the colored lakes of Kelimutu Volcano. Visitors usually visit early in the morning but our thinking was: walk up now if it was clear (it wasn't) since there is never a guarantee that you'll **see** the lakes. No one has to tell us about rising early in the morning for sunrises, lakes, craters and whatever else! Every one has always been a "no show" thanks to clouds or rain, while we stood, freezing to death, in the early morning air.

This was getting very depressing.

The drive continued past a small village of Leo people in Detasuko where one house and a "sitting grave" was visible from the road. Way back when, people were buried in a **sitting position**.

The Colored Lakes of Kelimutu Volcano

Why **bother** coming to Moni? For the multicolored lakes of Kelimutu Volcano. On a **clear day**, the three crater lakes change color due to varying mineral content in the water. The colors can be blue, green and red, or even turquoise. One never knows. Once an important spot for rituals, people believed souls of the dead found their last resting place in these lakes: old men in one lake, young men in another, and witches in the last lake. Tourists usually head up the mountain around 4:00a to see the sunrise over the lakes. There is a road up from Moni to a car park. From that point, you walk up stairs to the highest lookout point where all three lakes are visible.

You can also walk down to Moni through small villages from the top of Kelimutu which takes around 2-1/2 hours. The village is strung along the road to Maumere and perhaps your visit will coincide with the Monday Market in Moni

Please, listen to this advice. Tourists have a better chance of winning the **lottery** than seeing a sunrise over the multicolored lakes of Kelimutu Volcano. You must be...lucky, lucky, lucky. The **best chance** of seeing them is to stay **two nights**, watch the weather, and get up at 4:00a to see if the mountain is in fog. If so, go back to sleep and wait until afternoon. Watch to see if clouds have disappeared and, if so, hightail it up the mountain. We talked it over with Ricardos and told him to wake us immediately if the morning dawned clear. I awoke at 5:00a, looked out at cloud-covered mountains and went back to sleep.

A Singapore couple in the room next to us did make the trip up Kelimutu and got a brief view of the lakes before clouds rolled in again. They sat around freezing for another hour before giving up and came down the mountain.

The Hidayah Hotel in Moni

The driver pulled up in front of the most uninspiring hotel to date; the Hidayah with six-rooms, next to the main road, and the second best in Moni. The room was clean, electricity wouldn't go on until 6:00p, so we sat in this dark room, sulking. The bathroom also had the most unusual spigot I've ever seen, **laying on its side**. 'Tis a puzzlement...

Dinner at a restaurant close to the Hidayah for, what else, rice and noodles. We did try to order *gado-gado* but the electricity was off and the cook couldn't use a **blender** to mash peanuts for the peanut sauce. Whatever happened to do-it-yourself?

Making Copra

One last day in Flores began with a decent breakfast of black coffee, pancakes and dish of fruit before leaving for Maumere. Ricardos hoped to be in Maumere by noon to swing by the airport for a new e-ticket after quite a few conversations with Batavia Air who suggested doing this to avoid problems. **Proactive** trumps **reactive** when traveling.

There were "Three little pigs" walking along the road and amazing pig sties. These pigs (or a domesticated wild boar) are kept in wooden sheds on **stilts** along the highway and allowed out only occasionally. Pigs are eaten, sold and used for special **sacrificial ceremonies**. The Flores people may be Catholic but still persist in their animist beliefs.

Pigs are social animals and highly intelligent. One immediately came to the bars of its cage to see what was going on when I walked over. These grayish, black pigs/boars had long snouts and were unlike any that we've ever seen. Ricardos told me that pigs even lived in **caves** around here; they burrow into a mountainside to create a shady, daytime area. A minute after those words were spoken, I shouted, "Stop." A huge pig was resting in his cave while a few feet away, another relaxed in a mud bath!

Men along the road skewered fish, before grilling and selling to local drivers. A big local market was followed by a long stretch of road where women sat on the ground doing **something** with coconuts. I asked Ricardos to stop for a closer look when he said they were making **Copra**, whatever that was.

Several women sat in the grass, hacking coconuts into pieces with a machete, and prying out the white meat. Piles of white coconut meat in one area, pieces of coconut drying on mats, and even more stacks of just the coconut husk. Neighbors from other houses turned up, and a few cars stopped to see why two "Bulay" (white person/albino) were standing there. Tourists may wave to people while driving along the road but **never** stop to interact. It's difficult to explain what a big moment this was for them.

Copra is the dried meat, or kernel, of the coconut. Coconut oil is extracted to be widely used in cooking, certain medicines, and feed livestock. Piles of coconut **husks** are sold to restauranteurs who believe they imparts a delicious taste to *satays*; others use the husks for fuel. Making copra involves removing the shell, and breaking up the white meat to dry in the sun, the easiest method in the tropics. All you need is a mat to place coconut meat on facing the sky, either still in the shell, or pried out to dry (the more laborious version). Copra can also be dried by smoke or in kilns. These women were doing both: digging out the white meat; and switching to drying pieces naturally when they tired.

Locals then sell the Copra to companies who extract coconut oil with oil expellers. Ricardos spoke to a young man and the next thing we knew, he was shimmying up a coconut palm to knock down a few coconuts that fell with loud thuds. One of those falling babies could **kill** a person.

The local gave a fast whack with his machete, cut it in half, drank the coconut milk and began scraping pieces of fresh coconut out for us to taste. I found it amazing that they don't eat the white coconut pieces like we do, or even shred it to sell for cooking. They only eat the **innermost layer** of a young coconut. Ricardos bought two to go as a good will gesture, ingeniously tied together with pieces peeled back on each husk. I tried to do a bicep curl with two, heavy coconuts and couldn't get them past my elbow.

FYI: Copra is classed as a dangerous good due to its spontaneously combustive nature. Can you picture an **exploding coconut**?

We left the little Copra mom-and-pop industry behind; locals still laughing, excited over a once-in-a-lifetime encounter that none of us will ever forget.

Maumere

A stop at the Maumere airport to reconfirm e-tickets with Batavia Air before a fast look at Maumere itself. We obsessed throughout the trip about the flight from Maumere to Denpasar being cancelled; a common Indonesian occurrence, and one that Happy Trails warned about. Considering their cancellation advice, we had allowed an extra day for Maumere-Denpasar, another day for Denpasar-Singapore, before flying from Singapore-Chicago on yet another day. A cancellation would set off a **big** chain reaction, and could have meant an extra night in **Maumere**. The sweet Batavia Air representative assured us they **never** cancel flights. If everything goes according to plan, we'll then need a hotel in Bali, and an **extra night** in Singapore before flying back to America. No wonder we were stressed.

Maumere is the center of Sikkanese language and culture, and of Catholic activity since Portuguese Dominicans arrived 400 years ago. However, there's nothing of importance to see, Internet was excruciatingly slow (I finally gave up in disgust), and the one and only souvenir cum antique shop had **nothing** of interest. It certainly didn't help that the woman in the shop didn't speak English and couldn't tell us anything about any items.

Hotel Wailiti
The Hotel Wailiti (hotel-wailiti.com) was located outside central Maumere on the sea, and had several cottages in a lush, green garden with swimming pool. Situated on a beautiful stretch of calm beach, again, there was **nothing to sit on**. They gave us a little cottage facing the swimming pool. The hotel was clean, air conditioned, had hot water (if you waited long enough), and good food. Goodbyes to Ricardos and Nikolas, our last set of Lesser Sundra Island guides and drivers. Hotel Wailiti would transport us to the airport.

Leaving Flores Island
Checked in with Batavia Airlines who allowed 20 kilos/42 pounds of luggage per person, and carefully **weighed** each piece before hand-loading on the plane. Paid the usual domestic departure tax; through security where we **did not** have to take out computers, and liquids were allowed. Our flight arrived in Maumere only 30 minutes late and was quickly turned around. Almost all intra-Indonesia flights make more than one stop on routes, and today was no exception. Less than one hour to Kupang, Timor where the majority of passengers got off and transit people stayed on. The plane filled up with more passengers and took off for the 1-1/2 flight to Denpasar, Bali. After Denpasar, this flight would continue to Surabaya, finishing in Jakarta.

INDONESIAN FOOD

Cuisine consists of vegetables, chicken and fish with rice, the staple food throughout Indonesia. The most **popular** dishes are:

Nasi Goreng - Leftover rice, stir-fried with whatever ingredients the cook has on hand; shrimp, meat, vegetables, and topped with a fried egg.

Sate/Satay - A dish of marinated, skewered and grilled meat, usually served with a spicy peanut sauce (my favorite). Any meat will do: chicken, goat, beef, pork, fish...even a **King Cobra Satay** can be on the menu.

Soto - A common Indonesian soup infused with turmeric, made with chicken, beef or mutton.

Lumpia - Fried or steamed spring rolls served with a soybean sauce or sweet garlic sauce.

Pecel - A salad of boiled vegetables, dressed in a peanut-based spicy sauce. It is usually served as an accompaniment to rice. A peanut or dried fish/shrimp cracker (*rempeyek*) is served on the side.

Gado-gado (literal translation is "mix-mix") - Considered a one-dish meal, shredded and chopped green vegetables, fried tofu, boiled potatoes, hard cooked eggs are coated in a peanut sauce, served with white rice and garnished with shrimp crackers.

Noodles. Soft, hard, spicy, bland. Noodles in every incarnation.

Fresh fruits, grated coconut desserts and wonderful bakeries took care of my sweet tooth in Java.

HINDSIGHT IS 20/20

Timor, with a very interesting culture, also belongs to the Lesser Sundra Islands. We didn't have enough time to visit and, truthfully, have heard that there is little infrastructure.

Lombok. Focus on Lombok for R&R, beaches, partying on Gili Islands, snorkeling, diving, and to climb Mount Rinjani. Spend only one day on cultural sights around Mataram and that's Lombok;

Sumbawa was a big miss. I would have eliminated that gruesome, nothing drive across the island and done the below beginning in the recommended direction;

Komodo and Rinca Islands are definitely worth doing for a chance to see the Komodo Dragons, the world's largest lizard; **fly** to Labuan Bajo, Flores first, boat to the dragon islands, end in Sape, and fly back to Lombok or Bali from there. The smart and easy way; and

Flores Island. Go for snorkeling, diving, volcano climbing, Spider Rice Fields, and Bajawa. The island is lush; scenery became monotonous.

What did we like **best** about the **Lesser Sundra Islands**?

Lack of communication with the outer world! How wonderful to be totally disconnected with no telephones in rooms, no newspapers, no English television, and infrequent Internet;

Interaction with the locals. High school students in Bima; Copra women; children attending Easter Sunday Church services; and local wedding in Lombok;

Three impressive **sights**: **Puri Lingsar Temple**, Lombok; **Komodo Dragons** and boat journey; **Luba and Bena Villages** in Flores; and

Indonesian food. Our favorite *gado-gado* whenever a cook felt ambitious enough to pound peanuts into a paste. However, we were both getting a little tired of rice and noodles.

Now you know before you go! We've explored: Kalimantan (Borneo), Java, Bali, Sulawesi, Lombok, Sumbawa, Komodo, Rinca, and Flores which still leaves...**Sumatra, Timor and Irian Jaya** on my personal to-do list. **How about you?**

Other Travel Guides by Sheila Simkin:

Sheila's 25 Best China Travel Tips
Sheila's 25 Best India Travel Tips
Sheila's 25 Best International Layover Hotels

Sheila's Guide to Albania
Sheila's Guide to Cairo
Sheila's Guide to Egypt Desert Travel
Sheila's Guide to European Train Travel

Sheila's Guide to Guizhou, China

Sheila's Guide to Gujarat, India
Sheila's Guide to Ladakh, India
Sheila's Guide to Orissa, India
Sheila's Guide to Zanskar, Ladakh, India

Sheila's Guide to Sulawesi, Indonesia

Sheila's Guide to Myanmar/Burma

Sheila's Guide to North Ethiopia
Sheila's Guide to Tribal South Ethiopia
Sheila's Guide to Unknown Ethiopia
Sheila's Guide to River Kwai Area, Thailand

Sheila's Guide to Fast & Easy Antalya
Sheila's Guide to Fast & Easy Bali, Indonesia
Sheila's Guide to Fast & Easy Bangkok
Sheila's Guide to Fast & Easy Beijing
Sheila's Guide to Fast & Easy Buenos Aires
Sheila's Guide to Fast & Easy Chiang Mai
Sheila's Guide to Fast & Easy Hanoi
Sheila's Guide to Fast & Easy Istanbul
Sheila's Guide to Fast & Easy Java, Indonesia
Sheila's Guide to Fast & Easy Kolkata
Sheila's Guide to Fast & Easy Manila
Sheila's Guide to Fast & Easy Nile Cruises
Sheila's Guide to Fast & Easy Shanghai
Sheila's Guide to Fast & Easy Singapore

Discover Ancient Thai Kingdoms: AYUTTHAYA, SUKHOTHAI AND LAMPANG

Made in the USA
San Bernardino, CA
25 May 2013